THE UNITED STATES

12 ZACHARY TAYLOR

13 MILLARD FILLMORE

14 FRANKLIN PIERCE

15 JAMES BUCHANAN

16 ABRAHAM LINCOLN

17 ANDREW JOHNSON

18 ULYSSES S. GRANT

19 RUTHERFORD B. HAYES

20 JAMES GARFIELD

21 CHESTER A. ARTHUR

22 GROVER CLEVELAND

Jeopardy! champion and *New York Times* bestselling author

KEN JENNINGS'

JUNIOR GENIUS GUIDES

U.S. PRESIDENTS

BY **KEN JENNINGS**

ILLUSTRATED BY **MIKE LOWERY**

SEMPER QUAERENS

LITTLE SIMON

New York London Toronto Sydney New Delhi

THE OFFICIAL
JUNIOR GENIUS CIPHER

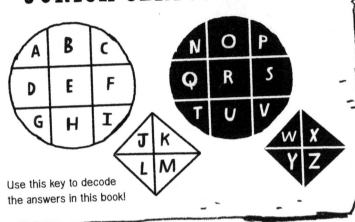

Use this key to decode
the answers in this book!

LITTLE SIMON
An imprint of Simon & Schuster Children's Publishing Division
1230 Avenue of the Americas, New York, New York 10020
Text copyright © 2014 by Ken Jennings
Illustrations copyright © 2014 by Simon & Schuster, Inc.
All rights reserved, including the right of reproduction in whole or in part in any form.
LITTLE SIMON is a registered trademark of Simon & Schuster, Inc., and associated colophon is a
trademark of Simon & Schuster, Inc.
For information about special discounts for bulk purchases, please contact Simon & Schuster Special Sales
at 1-866-506-1949 or business@simonandschuster.com.
The Simon & Schuster Speakers Bureau can bring authors to your live event. For more information or to
book an event contact the Simon & Schuster Speakers Bureau at 1-866-248-3049 or visit our website at
www.simonspeakers.com.
Manufactured in China 0214 SCP
First Edition 2 4 6 8 10 9 7 5 3 1
Library of Congress Cataloging-in-Publication Data
Jennings, Ken, 1974–
U.S. Presidents / By Ken Jennings ; Illustrated by Mike Lowery. — First Edition.
pages cm. — (Ken Jennings' Junior Genius Guides)
Includes bibliographical references and index.
ISBN 978-1-4424-9850-1 (hardcover : alk. paper) — ISBN 978-1-4424-7332-4 (pbk. : alk. paper) —
ISBN 978-1-4424-7333-1 (ebook) 1. Presidents—United States—Biography—Miscellanea—Juvenile
literature. 2. Presidents—United States—Miscellanea—Juvenile literature. I. Lowery, Mike, 1980–
illustrator. II. Title.
E176.1.J46 2014
973.09'9—dc23
[B]
2013023737

CONTENTS

INTRODUCTION

Settle down, class, the bell has rung. I'm Professor Jennings, your gentleman-scholar-in-residence. As always, I'll be spending the day scooping out buckets of cool, refreshing information for your thirsty minds from my bottomless pool of knowledge.

Today we're going to meet one of the most elite clubs in the world: the forty-three men who have been president of the United States of America. I know, you think you already know about the presidents. You've seen them  on money. You might have played with the toys they inspired, like teddy bears or Lincoln Logs. Just walking around your neighborhood, you might pass streets or schools named for presidents. But how much do we really know about them? Do you know which chief executive had a pet pygmy hippo? Which one saw a UFO? Which one was afraid of light switches? After today's class, you will.

The presidency is an exclusive club, but we Junior Geniuses are not. Anyone can join—as long as they like to learn cool stuff. So let's begin with the Junior Genius Pledge. Everyone: Please stand up facing the drawing of Einstein, put your right index finger to your temple, and repeat after me.

With all my fellow Junior Geniuses, I solemnly pledge to quest after questions, to angle for answers, to seek out, and to soak up. I will hunger and thirst for knowledge my whole life through, and I dedicate my discoveries to all humankind, with trivia not for just us, but for all.

Very good! Let's all turn to page 6 and begin.

FIRST PERIOD

The Highest Office in the Land

After winning the Revolutionary War, General George Washington probably could have had anything he wanted. Some of his army officers suggested he should be crowned king. If Washington had agreed to be king, and the crown had been passed down to his heirs, do you know who would be running America today? Paul Emery Washington, of San Antonio, Texas, retired regional manager of a building-supply company!

Luckily, Washington didn't want to be king, and instead, in 1789, he was elected and sworn in as the first president of the United States. For the last 225 years, instead of "His Majesty," we've referred to our head of state as just plain "Mr. President." (And maybe, someday soon, "Madam President.")

MAYBE THIS SHOULD BE THE HANSON MONUMENT IN HANSON, D.C.

Strictly speaking, Washington wasn't the first American president—he was the ninth! Before the Constitution was ratified, eight different men presided over the Continental Congress. If you count these guys, America's *real* first president was a Maryland tobacco planter named John Hanson.

But even though the United States is a democracy, the president still gets plenty of pomp and ceremony. In this chapter, we'll take a look at some of the traditions and trappings that have grown up over the centuries around the highest office in the land.

Big Bird

The bald eagle on the official presidential seal holds both a bundle of arrows and an olive branch, to symbolize the president's leadership in war *and* peace. Many people believe that the eagle is redrawn to face the arrows during times of war, but you should know better, Junior Geniuses. That's just a myth.

The seal has lots of hidden thirteens, to symbolize the thirteen original states of the union.

If you watch the president on TV, you'll see the seal printed everywhere he goes. The Mars candy company even puts the seal on special presidential boxes of M&M's, available only at the White House and on Air Force One.

1600 Pennsylvania Avenue

George Washington never lived in the White House! It took ten years to build the city now named for him, so Washington governed from executive mansions in New York and Philadelphia instead.

John Adams moved into the White House in November 1800 as its paint was still drying. Not a single room was completed, and the First Family used the large East Room, where ceremonies and receptions are held today, to hang their laundry. The day after moving in, Adams wrote to his wife, Abigail:

> "I Pray Heaven to Bestow the Best of Blessings on This House and All that shall hereafter inhabit it. May none but Honest and Wise Men ever rule under this Roof!"

Today these words appear above the fireplace in the White House State Dining Room.

The Adams family even had to use an outhouse, as the White House had no indoor bathrooms or running water! But don't worry about the president today having to run out to the Rose Garden in the middle of the night when he feels the call of nature. Since 1800, the mansion has been renovated many times with all the latest conveniences:

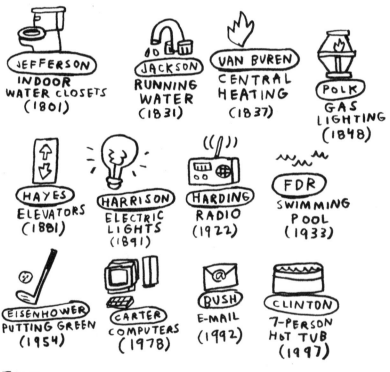

JEFFERSON
INDOOR
WATER CLOSETS
(1801)

JACKSON
RUNNING
WATER
(1831)

VAN BUREN
CENTRAL
HEATING
(1837)

POLK
GAS
LIGHTING
(1848)

HAYES
ELEVATORS
(1881)

HARRISON
ELECTRIC
LIGHTS
(1891)

HARDING
RADIO
(1922)

FDR
SWIMMING
POOL
(1933)

EISENHOWER
PUTTING GREEN
(1954)

CARTER
COMPUTERS
(1978)

BUSH
E-MAIL
(1992)

CLINTON
7-PERSON
HOT TUB
(1997)

Extra Credit

Even before he got into hot water, Richard Nixon wasn't much of a swimmer. In 1969, he ordered FDR's pool covered up to expand the White House pressroom. His successor, Gerald Ford, promptly had a new outdoor pool dug in the South Lawn.

Today the White House has 6 levels, 132 rooms, 28 fireplaces, 147 windows, 35 bathrooms, a bowling alley, and a movie theater. Even with all that space, things can get crowded. President James Buchanan used to invite over so many houseguests that he once wound up sleeping on the floor in a hallway!

All that luxury isn't free, however. Every president gets a monthly bill from the White House and is expected to pay all his family's costs, everything from groceries to toiletries to dry cleaning. And the staff says that new presidents always complain about the cost!

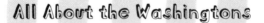

All About the Washingtons

George Washington, one of the richest Americans of his time, thought that the president shouldn't get paid at all, but instead just have his expenses reimbursed. Congress disagreed, and voted a $25,000 salary for the president. At the time, that was 2 percent of the national budget—the equivalent of $76 *billion* today! Today's presidential salary: $400,000 a year. Not bad, for government work.

The Earpiece Corps

When you see Secret Service agents on TV talking into their sleeves (actually a small microphone on their wrists) what are they saying? Often they use code words, like

"POTUS" (**P**resident **o**f **t**he **U**nited **S**tates) and "FLOTUS" (**F**irst **L**ady **o**f **t**he **U**nited **S**tates). All modern presidents have had their own individual code names as well. Here's a top secret look behind the sunglasses.

	PRESIDENT	FIRST LADY	CHILDREN
Kennedy	Lancer	Lace	Lyric and Lark
Johnson	Volunteer	Victoria	Velvet and Venus
Nixon	Searchlight	Starlight	Sugarfoot and Sunbonnet
Ford	Passkey	Pinafore	Professor, Packman, Panda
Carter	Deacon	Dancer	Derby, Deckhand, Diamond, Dynamo
Reagan	Rawhide	Rainbow	Rhyme, Riddler, Ribbon, Reliant
Bush 41	Timberwolf	Tranquility	Trailblazer, Tripper, Trapline, Tuner
Clinton	Eagle	Evergreen	Energy
Bush 43	Trailblazer	Tempo	Turquoise and Twinkle
Obama	Renegade	Renaissance	Radiance and Rosebud

In an epic example of bad timing, Abraham Lincoln signed the law that created the Secret Service on April 14, 1865—the same day he was shot. But the Secret Service was actually formed as a branch of the Department of the Treasury, mostly to fight counterfeiting. They didn't take on their most famous duty—protecting the president and other VIPs—until after the McKinley assassination in 1901.

Back then, security wasn't such a big deal. Calvin Coolidge used to enjoy giving his security detail the slip and going for walks by himself out on F Street. But today, the president receives more than thirty death threats *every day*, so his protection has to be airtight.

Every president back to Reagan has had an official food tester who tastes every dish served, to make sure it's not poisoned. (If the food tester isn't there, POTUS can't eat lunch.) In 2007, Austrian newspapers even reported that during a state visit to Vienna, President Bush used a special toilet that collected his waste. The toilet was flown back to the U.S., making sure that no poop was left behind!

The president often wears bulletproof protection under his suit, and his car is equipped with smoke grenades, tear gas, its own oxygen supply, a firefighting system, and a blood bank in the trunk equipped with the president's blood type.

Road Trip

Nowadays, the president can't just hop on his horse and ride to church alone, the way Lincoln did. When POTUS goes anywhere today, it's a pretty big project. Here's what his motorcade looks like.

ROUTE CAR
Five minutes ahead

PILOT CAR
One minute ahead

LEAD CARS
Guide the motorcade

SPARE CAR
Decoy of the

STAGECOACH
The president's car

HALFBACK
The Secret Service detail

CLASSIFIED
? ? ?

CONTROL
Key staff

SUPPORT
Key staff

CAT
The presidential counterassult team

ID CAR
Countersurveillance

CLASSIFIED
? ? ?

PRESS VANS
Reporters

ROADRUNNER
The White House Communications Agency

AMBULANCE

Many presidents grow to have close relationships with their security.

• **EISENHOWER,** who loved to golf, got tired of squirrels tearing up the White House putting green, so he tasked his Secret Service with drawing up a countermeasure called Operation Squirrel Seduction.

• **RONALD REAGAN,** in retirement and suffering from Alzheimer's disease, loved to spend his days skimming leaves off his pool. He didn't know his agents were carefully replacing all the leaves, so he'd always have some to remove!

• **BEST OF ALL, GERALD FORD** used to blame the Secret Service whenever he passed gas—which was often. "Did you do that?" he would ask loudly. "Show some class!" His agents must not have minded. One of them even wound up marrying his daughter, Susan!

NO DIVING

Prank of America

All this security doesn't *always* work perfectly. In 2007, an Icelandic high school student named Vifill Atlason phoned the White House pretending to be the president of Iceland, and managed to schedule a meeting with President Bush before his hoax was discovered!

Frequent Flier

In 1945, Franklin Roosevelt became the first commander in chief ever to travel in a special presidential airplane, when he flew to the Soviet Union to attend the Yalta Conference in a plane called the Sacred Cow. Today, any plane with the president on board gets a cooler call sign: Air Force One.

There are currently two Boeing 747s in the president's fleet. These are no ordinary passenger jets—they each have lots of special accommodations for the

president, including a workout room, a five-chef galley that can serve two thousand meals, and a mini-hospital. The planes can also be refueled in midair, so the president can keep flying indefinitely in case of a national emergency. He'd never be out of touch with Washington, since each plane has state-of-the-art communication equipment, including 85 phones and 19 televisions. In total, its instruments use 238 *miles* of wiring. Air Force One is even specially shielded to withstand a nuclear strike!

Pop Quiz!

Near the end of his second term, James Madison burned out on Washington and spent *four full months* just chilling at his Virginia estate. What's the modern name for the president's private retreat, which was called Shangri-La until President Eisenhower renamed it in 1953 after his grandson?

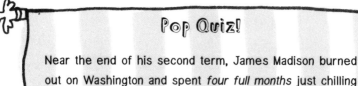

To-Do List

Some presidential traditions happen every year. Here's a helpful calendar, in case you're ever elected. (Not for a few more years, though. The Constitution says the president has to be at least thirty-five.)

The State of the Union Address

The Constitution says that the president "shall from time to time give to Congress information of the State of the Union." Thomas Jefferson *hated* public speaking (some historians think he might have had a stutter), so he used to just write Congress a letter. But ever since Woodrow Wilson, presidents have given their annual update as a speech to a joint session of Congress. Every year, the whole Cabinet attends the speech—except for one "designated survivor," who is taken to a secret location. That way, if there's some emergency, at least one person in line to succeed to the presidency is still safe.

THE PRESIDENTIAL LINE OF SUCCESSION

PRESIDENT

VICE PRESIDENT

SPEAKER OF THE HOUSE

PRESIDENT PRO TEMPORE OF THE SENATE

SECRETARY OF STATE

SECRETARY OF THE TREASURY

SECRETARY OF DEFENSE

ATTORNEY GENERAL

The Easter Egg Roll

Families used to enjoy Easter picnics on the Capitol lawn, but they were so hard on the lawn that Congress passed a Turf Protection Law in 1876 to keep kids off the Capitol grass. When President Rutherford B. Hayes heard about the ban from some unhappy children (including his own!) he decided to open up the White House lawn to egg rollers. Since then,  the White House has traditionally hosted egg-themed festivities the Monday after Easter, with as many as thirty thousand people crowding the lawn.

The First Pitch

In 1910, the owner of baseball's Washington Senators convinced President Taft to attend the team's opening game. Before the game, Taft tossed the ball from the

stands to pitcher Walter Johnson, who later went on to become one of the founding members of the Baseball Hall of Fame. Today, presidents get to throw from the actual pitcher's mound. STEEE-RIKE!

The Turkey Pardon

In 1865, President Lincoln was presented with a plump turkey for the Christmas dinner table, but his twelve-year-old son Tad pleaded for the turkey's life, so Lincoln agreed to spare it. In 1989, the first President Bush began the tradition of issuing an informal presidential "pardon" to one lucky turkey every Thanksgiving. The pardoned turkey gets sent

back to the turkey farm, to George Washington's Mount Vernon estate, or even to Disneyland! Sadly, most of the turkeys don't live too long after their reprieve. One pardoned bird keeled over the very next day! Pass the gravy.

The Christmas Tree Lighting

Many presidents have decked the White House halls with holiday cheer. Teddy Roosevelt offered Santa-shaped ice-cream sculptures to his young guests. Andrew Jackson gave the kids exploding cotton "snowballs" and held impromptu snowball fights in the White House dining room! But the first White House Christmas tree was decorated in 1889 by Benjamin Harrison's family, who used candles. (Kids: This is a fire hazard! Do not try this at home! Or Benjamin Harrison's ghost will come down your chimney and leave you coal in your stocking.)

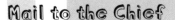

Mail to the Chief

Do you like checking the mail, hoping to see an envelope with your name on it? The president of the United States gets fifteen thousand letters every day! His friends have to be issued a top secret nine-digit ZIP code to use so their personal mail doesn't get lost in the shuffle.

Among the mail, there are hundreds of gifts sent to the White House from fans across the country and around the world. Here are some of the weirdest gifts a U.S. president has ever received:

- **The largest watermelon in Georgia.** In 1897, the state of Georgia sent William McKinley a prizewinning seventy-eight-pound melon, wrapped in the state flag.

- **A Komodo dragon.** The Indonesian government thought George H. W. Bush should have Naga, a nine-foot-long carnivorous lizard.

- **Raw lamb meat.** The president of Argentina gave the second President Bush three hundred pounds of lamb meat! He should have fed it to his dad's Komodo dragon.

• **Presidential portraits you could fit up your nose.** A Pakistani fan of Richard Nixon's carved two intricate portraits of the thirty-seventh president—on grains of rice.

• **Crocodile insurance.** In Darwin, Australia, Barack Obama was presented with $50,000 of insurance in case of a crocodile attack. "My wife, Michelle, will be relieved," he said.

• **A coffee-table-size cheese.** Andrew Jackson once received a wheel of cheddar cheese four feet in diameter from a New York dairy farmer. When the giant cheese began smelling up the White House, Jackson rolled it into the lobby and held a public reception. Ten thousand guests stopped by to finish it off.

SECOND PERIOD

Class of 43

It's time to meet all forty-three of the men who have been president of the United States. That's right, Junior Geniuses: Even though Barack Obama is the forty-fourth president, he's actually the forty-*third* person to hold the office. According to an official ruling by the State Department, Grover Cleveland is both the twenty-second *and* the twenty-fourth president, because his two terms weren't consecutive.

Homework

Ask a grown-up, "How is it that the twenty-second and twenty-fourth U.S. presidents had the same parents, but weren't brothers?" Bet you stump them!

Most of the presidents, of course, were from different eras and didn't know each other. They don't all hang out together, like the robot presidents do at Disney World. But what if they *were* all friends, like a big school class? If so, the yearbook of Presidents High might look something like this.

1

GEORGE WASHINGTON

Feb. 22, 1732–Dec. 14, 1799

"The Father of His Country"

Term: 1789–1797

"I hold the maxim no less applicable to public than to private affairs, that honesty is always the best policy."

 **Federalist**

Activities Surveying, foxhunting, winning the Revolutionary War

Most Likely to Be a Fashion Designer When he commanded Virginia's militia, Washington insisted on designing their stylish, color-coordinated uniforms himself!

2

JOHN ADAMS

Oct. 30, 1735–July 4, 1826

"The Colossus of Independence," "His Rotundity"

Term: 1797–1801

"Our obligations to our country never cease but with our lives."

Federalist

Activities Law, diplomacy, independence, reading, fishing

Least Popular Lawyer In 1770, Adams agreed to defend the British soldiers accused of the infamous Boston Massacre, because he thought they deserved a fair trial. Six were acquitted.

3

THOMAS JEFFERSON

April 13, 1743–July 4, 1826

"The Sage of Monticello"

Term: 1801–1809

"We hold these truths to be self-evident, that all men are created equal."

🌿 **Democratic-Republican** 🌿

Activities Writing, architecture, science, inventing, violin playing

Sneakiest Architect
It was discovered in 1930 that Jefferson had entered the design contest for the White House using the pseudonym "A.Z." When he lost, he never told anyone.

4

JAMES MADISON

Mar. 16, 1751–June 28, 1836

"Father of the Constitution," "Little Jemmy"

Term: 1809–1817

"The happy Union of these States is a wonder; their Constitution a miracle; their example the hope of Liberty throughout the world."

🌿 **Democratic-Republican** 🌿

Activities The Federalist Papers, the Constitution, chess, standing on chairs to reach things

Busiest Ghostwriter Madison wrote most of George Washington's first inaugural address. He also wrote Congress's reply to the speech and Washington's reply to the reply!

5

JAMES MONROE

April 28, 1758–July 4, 1831

"The Last Cocked Hat"

Term: 1817–1825

"National honor is the national property of the highest value."

🌿**Democratic-Republican**🌿

Activities Government service (seven high offices!), horseback riding

Most Likely to Show Up on a Map of Africa The capital of the African nation of Liberia is Monrovia, named for Monroe, who helped found the colony for freed slaves.

6

JOHN QUINCY ADAMS

July 11, 1767–Feb. 23, 1848

"Old Man Eloquent"

Term: 1825–1829

"Always vote for principle, though you may vote alone, and you may cherish the sweetest reflection that your vote is never lost."

🌿**Democratic-Republican**🌿

Activities Diplomacy, abolition, billiards, astronomy

Smallest Swimsuit Collection Quincy Adams enjoyed skinny-dipping every morning at 5 a.m. in the chilly Potomac River. One morning, a reporter sat on his clothes and refused to leave until he granted her an interview!

7

ANDREW JACKSON

> Mar. 15, 1767–Jun. 8, 1845

"Old Hickory"

Term: 1829–1837

"One man with courage makes a majority."

 Democrat

Activities Indian wars, dismantling the national bank, horse racing, cock fighting

Coolest Under Pressure
Jackson fought more than one hundred duels, including one with Charles Dickinson, an expert marksman. Jackson knew he had to aim carefully, but this gave Dickinson the first shot. Jackson took a bullet near his heart that broke a couple of ribs, calmly returned fire, and won the duel.

8

MARTIN VAN BUREN

> Dec. 5, 1782–July 24, 1862

"Old Kinderhook,"
"The Little Magician"

Term: 1837–1841

"It is easier to do a job right than to explain why you didn't."

 **Democrat**

Activities Patronage, Indian resettlement, opera, wine, gambling

Exchange Student
Van Buren was the only president who spoke English as a second language. As a boy, he was raised speaking Dutch.

9

WILLIAM HENRY HARRISON

> Feb. 9, 1773–April 4, 1841

"Tippecanoe"

Term: 1841 (31 days)

"The strongest of all governments is that which is most free."

 Whig

Activities The army, Bible reading, dying

Most Likely to Steal Your Daughter Anna Harrison's father, a stern judge, hated Harrison and refused to let them date. The two hastily married in 1795 while the judge was away on business.

10

JOHN TYLER

> Mar. 29, 1790–Jan. 18, 1862

"His Accidency"

Term: 1841–1845

"Popularity, I have always thought, may aptly be compared to a coquette—the more you woo her, the more apt is she to elude your embrace."

 Whig

Activities Law, fathering lots of children, the Confederacy, the violin, foxhunting

Worst Bird Breeder Tyler owned a canary named for himself, Johnny Ty. Poor Johnny Ty died shortly after the Tylers tried to pair him with another canary—who also turned out to be male.

11

JAMES K. POLK

Nov. 2, 1795–Jun. 15, 1849

"Napoleon of the Stump,"
"Young Hickory"

Term: 1845–1849

"With me it is emphatically true that the Presidency is 'no bed of roses.'"

🌿 Democrat 🌿

Activities Working, not having fun, working more

Biggest Buzzkill The Polks were religiously strict and banned dancing, card playing, and liquor from the White House. At his inaugural ball, all dancing and music stopped as soon as the Polks arrived, and resumed once they'd left.

12

ZACHARY TAYLOR

Nov. 24, 1784–Jul. 9, 1850

"Old Rough and Ready"

Term: 1849–1850

"The idea that I should become President seems to me too visionary to require a serious answer. It has never entered my head, nor is it likely to enter the head of any other person."

🌿 Whig 🌿

Activities The military, the spoils system, precision tobacco spitting

Most Likely to Stiff the Mailman at Christmas Taylor refused to pay the postage due on the 1848 letter notifying him that he'd been nominated as president, so he didn't learn about the news for several days.

13

MILLARD FILLMORE

> Jan. 7, 1800–Mar. 8, 1874

"Millard Fillmore"

Term: 1850–1853

"An honorable defeat is better than a dishonorable victory."

🌿 Whig 🌿

Activities Law, tariffs, the Fugitive Slave Act, collecting books

Class Bookworm The Fillmores owned forty thousand books and created the White House library. In 1851, he helped fight an accidental fire that destroyed two-thirds of the Library of Congress.

14

FRANKLIN PIERCE

> Nov. 23, 1804–Oct. 8, 1869

"Handsome Frank"

Term: 1853–1857

"With the Union my best and dearest earthly hopes are entwined."

🌿 Democrat 🌿

Activities The Kansas-Nebraska Act, defending slavery, alcoholism, fishing

Dateless Wonder Pierce served his whole term without a vice president around. His running mate, William Rufus King, died of tuberculosis in April 1853, after taking the oath of office and spending most of his time as vice president in Cuba for his health.

15

JAMES BUCHANAN

Apr. 23, 1791–Jun. 1, 1868

"Old Buck"

Term: 1857–1861

"I am the last President of the United States!"

 **Democrat**

Activities Bachelor life, card playing, failing to prevent the Civil War

Most Likely to Ride on His Pet Buchanan owned the largest dog ever to live in the White House, a 170-pound Newfoundland named Lara.

16

ABRAHAM LINCOLN

Feb. 12, 1809–Apr. 15, 1865

"Honest Abe," "The Great Emancipator"

Term: 1861–1865

"Now we are engaged in a great civil war, testing whether that nation or any nation so conceived and so dedicated, can long endure."

Republican

Activities Rail-splitting, storytelling, emancipation, theater

Most Likely to Succeed, Eventually Before becoming president, Abraham Lincoln lost his job, bankrupted his general store, was turned down for a general land office position, and lost two Senate races.

17

ANDREW JOHNSON

Dec. 29, 1808–Jul. 31, 1875

"The Tennessee Tailor"

Term: 1865–1869

"I feel incompetent to perform duties so important and responsible as those which have been so unexpectedly thrown upon me."

Republican

Activities Tailoring, checkers, gardening, circuses, Reconstruction

Most Wanted (Dead or Alive!) When he was sixteen, Johnson ran away from his job as an indentured servant to a tailor, and newspaper ads offered a ten-dollar reward for his return.

18

ULYSSES S. GRANT

Apr. 27, 1822–Jul. 23, 1885

"Unconditional Surrender"

Term: 1869–1877

"Although a soldier by profession, I have never felt any sort of fondness for war, and I have never advocated it, except as a means of peace."

Republican

Activities Winning the Civil War, cigar smoking, whittling, painting

Luckiest Double Dater Grant was supposed to accompany Lincoln to the play the night that Booth shot the president, and he may have been killed as well. He canceled at the last minute, because his wife didn't like Mary Todd Lincoln.

19
RUTHERFORD B. HAYES

Oct. 4, 1822–Jan. 17, 1893

"Old Granny," "Rutherfraud"

Term: 1877–1881

"He serves his party best who serves his country best."

 **Republican**

Activities Law, chess, landscaping, civil service reform

Most Likely to Finish an Obelisk Funding for the Washington Monument had stalled for more than fifteen years when Hayes took office, but he arranged for the money to finally complete the monument.

20
JAMES GARFIELD

Nov. 19, 1831–Sep. 19, 1881

"The Preacher President"

Term: 1881 (200 days)

"The president is the last person in the world to know what the people really want and think."

 **Republican**

Activities Religion, classical languages, hunting, juggling

Most Likely to Cover His Bets In the same election when he won the presidency, Garfield also retained his seat in the House of Representatives and won a Senate seat. For a brief period, he'd been elected to all three offices at once!

21

CHESTER A. ARTHUR

Oct. 5, 1829–Nov. 18, 1886

"The Dude President"

Term: 1881–1885

"Men may die, but the fabric of our free institutions remains unshaken."

🌿 **Republican** 🌿

Activities Shopping, parties, banjo playing

Most Devoted Widower Arthur's wife, Ellen, died shortly before his nomination as vice president. In her memory, he dedicated a stained-glass window to her at their church—and made sure it was on the side of the building where he could see it at night from the White House.

22, 24

GROVER CLEVELAND

Mar. 18, 1837–Jun. 24, 1908

"Uncle Jumbo," "Grover the Good"

Terms: 1885–1889 and 1893–1897

"Officeholders are the agents of the people, not their masters."

🌿 **Democrat** 🌿

Activities Law enforcement, fishing, billiards, eating meat

Future Movie Star Cleveland was a screen star before Ronald Reagan was even born! In 1895, he agreed to be filmed signing a bill into law for a scene in the hit "pictureplay," *A Capital Courtship.*

23

BENJAMIN HARRISON

Aug. 20, 1833–Mar. 13, 1901

"The Centennial President"

Term: 1889–1893

"The bud of victory is always in the truth."

🌿 **Republican** 🌿

Activities Law, the Civil War, duck hunting, the Sherman Antitrust Act

Most Likely to Sleep with a Light On Electricity was first installed in the White House in 1891, but the Harrisons were frightened of being electrocuted, and refused to touch the light switches.

25

WILLIAM MCKINLEY

Jan. 29, 1843–Sep. 14, 1901

"The Idol of Ohio"

Term: 1897–1901

"War should never be entered upon until every agency of peace has failed."

🌿 **Republican** 🌿

Activities Law, the theater, cribbage, the Spanish-American War

Most Likely to Fail at Geography When Admiral Dewey cabled McKinley to announce that he'd won the Philippines from Spain, the president had to check a globe. "I could not have told where those damned islands were within two thousand miles!" he admitted.

26

THEODORE ROOSEVELT

Oct. 27, 1858–Jan. 6, 1919

"Teddy,"
"The Lion,"
"The Rough Rider"

Term: 1901–1909

"Speak softly and carry a big stick."

 **Republican**

Activities Big-game hunting, judo, boxing, trust busting, conservation

Caffeine Addict Maxwell House coffee claims that Teddy Roosevelt coined its famous slogan "Good to the last drop" after finishing a cup while visiting Nashville in 1907.

27

WILLIAM HOWARD TAFT

Sep. 15, 1857–Mar. 8, 1930

"Big Bill"

Term: 1909–1913

"I love judges, and I love courts. They are my ideals, that typify on earth what we shall meet hereafter in heaven under a just God."

Republican

Activities Golf, baseball, eating, the judiciary

Unlikeliest Jock Despite his famous girth, Taft was an avid athlete and light-footed dancer. During a stop in Hawaii in 1900, he even tried surfing at Waikiki!

28

WOODROW WILSON

Dec. 28, 1856–Feb. 3, 1924

"The Schoolmaster"

Term: 1913–1921

"The world must be made safe for democracy."

 **Democrat**

Activities Academia, vaudeville, bridge, the League of Nations

Least Likely to Win a Beauty Contest Wilson's favorite limerick was "I know how I ugly I are. I know my face ain't no star. But I don't mind it, 'cause I'm behind it. The folks out in front get the jar!"

29

WARREN G. HARDING

Nov. 2, 1865–Aug. 2, 1923

"The Happy Hooligan"

Term: 1921–1923

"America's present need is not heroics, but healing; not nostrums, but normalcy."

Republican

Activities Journalism, poker, womanizing, sousaphone playing

Most Likely to Develop a Gambling Problem Harding once bet—and lost—a set of White House china on a hand of poker.

30

CALVIN COOLIDGE

Jul. 4, 1872–Jan. 5, 1933

"Silent Cal"

Term: 1923–1929

"I have never been hurt by what I have not said."

🌿 **Republican** 🌿

Activities Sleeping, mechanical-horse riding, harmonica playing, debt trimming

Shiniest Forehead One of Coolidge's favorite luxuries was to have his head rubbed with Vaseline while he ate breakfast in bed.

31

HERBERT HOOVER

Aug. 10, 1874–Oct. 20, 1964

"The Great Engineer"

Term: 1929–1933

"I am convinced we have now passed the worst and with continued unity of effort we shall rapidly recover."

🌿 **Republican** 🌿

Activities Mining, war relief, fishing, hiking

Least Popular Hoover was widely blamed for the Great Depression. Hobos called their newspapers "Hoover blankets"; empty pockets were "Hoover flags." In 1930, a sportswriter pointed out that Babe Ruth was making more than the president. "I know, but I had a better year," replied Ruth.

32

FRANKLIN D. ROOSEVELT

Jan. 30, 1882–April 12, 1945

"FDR"

Term: 1933–1945

"I pledge you, I pledge myself, to a new deal for the American people."

 **Democrat**

Activities Polio, stamp collecting, public works, Social Security

Worst DJ Roosevelt's theme song, "Happy Days Are Here Again," is still heard at Democratic Party gatherings today. Ironically, the song was published on the eve of the 1929 stock market crash—and was written by two staunch Republicans!

33

HARRY S. TRUMAN

May 8, 1884–Dec. 26, 1972

"Give 'Em Hell Harry"

Term: 1945–1953

"If you can't stand the heat, get out of the kitchen."

Democrat

Activities Men's retail, piano playing, swimming, the Korean War

Most Presidential Apartment
As a young man in Kansas City, Truman roomed with Dwight Eisenhower's brother Arthur, and the two remained friends even when Truman and Eisenhower became political rivals.

34

DWIGHT D. EISENHOWER

Oct. 14, 1890–Mar. 28, 1969

"Ike"

Term: 1953–1961

"A people that values its privileges above its principles soon loses both."

🌿 Republican 🌿

Activities Defeating the Nazis, golf, paint-by-number, integration

Most Likely to Have Incorrect "Most Likely to..." In his high school yearbook, Eisenhower was voted most likely to become a history professor. His brother Edgar was voted most likely to be president someday!

35

JOHN F. KENNEDY

May 29, 1917–Nov. 22, 1963

"JFK"

Term: 1961–1963

"We stand today on the edge of a New Frontier, the frontier of the 1960s. A frontier of unknown opportunities and perils, a frontier of unfulfilled hopes and threats."

🌿 Democrat 🌿

Activities Catholicism, touch football, the Cuban missile crisis, the space race

Least Likely to Be in His Own Portrait Aaron Shikler's famous presidential portrait of Kennedy looking down with his arms folded isn't even JFK! It was based on a photo of JFK's brother Ted looking down at Kennedy's grave site.

36

LYNDON B. JOHNSON

Aug. 27, 1908–Jan. 22, 1973

"LBJ," "Landslide Lyndon"

Term: 1963–1969

"I do not find it easy to send the flower of our youth, our finest young men, into battle."

🌿 Democrat 🌿

Activities Dominoes, ranching, Vietnam, civil rights

Most Likely to Save Money on Monogrammed Towels
Lyndon Baines Johnson made sure everyone in his family had the same set of initials. He and his wife, "Lady Bird," named their daughters Lynda Bird and Luci Baines. For a time, the Johnsons even had a dog named Little Beagle.

37

RICHARD M. NIXON

Jan. 9, 1913–April 22, 1994

"Tricky Dick"

Term: 1969–1974

"When the president does it, that means that it is not illegal."

🌿 Republican 🌿

Activities Anti-Communism, wiretapping, bowling, comebacks

Most Likely to Be on *Time*
Nixon appeared on the cover of *Time* magazine a whopping fifty-two times, more than any other person before or since.

38

GERALD R. FORD

Jul. 14, 1913–Dec. 26, 2006

"The Accidental President"

Term: 1974–1977

"Our long national nightmare is over."

🌿 Republican 🌿

Activities Football, skiing, inflation, pardons

Least Romantic Ford was running for Congress in October 1948 when he and his wife, Betty, were married. He actually ducked out of the rehearsal dinner to give a speech, and campaigned on his wedding day.

39

JAMES CARTER

October 1, 1924–

"The Peanut Farmer"

Term: 1977–1981

"Our commitment to human rights must be absolute, our laws fair, our natural beauty preserved."

🌿 Democrat 🌿

Activities Nuclear ("nucular") physics, tennis, Bible reading, humanitarian work

Most Afraid of Bunnies During a presidential fishing trip to Georgia in 1979, a swamp rabbit swam menacingly toward Carter's boat. "President Attacked by Rabbit!" announced a *Washington Post* headline.

40

RONALD REAGAN

Feb. 6, 1911–Jun. 5, 2004

"The Great Communicator,"
"The Gipper"

Term: 1981–1989

"We will become that shining city on a hill."

🌿 **Republican** 🌿

Activities Acting, tax cuts, horseback riding, naps

Least Helpful with Chores
In 1984, young Andy Smith wrote Reagan saying that his mom had declared his room a "disaster area," and asked if he could have some federal funds for the cleanup. Mindful as ever of government excess, Reagan wrote back that the official request would have to come from the agency that declared the disaster area— namely, Andy's mom.

41

GEORGE H. W. BUSH

June 12, 1924–

"Poppy,"
"41"

Term: 1989–1993

"I want a kinder and gentler nation."

🌿 **Republican** 🌿

Activities Oil, horseshoes, sailing, the Gulf War

Future Big Leaguer Bush captained the Yale baseball team that played in the very first College World Series in 1947. The next year, Bush was on deck in the ninth inning of the deciding game, with the bases loaded and nobody out. But the batter ahead of him hit into a rare triple play, ending the game.

42

WILLIAM J. CLINTON

August 19, 1946–

"Slick Willie,"
"The Comeback Kid"

Term: 1993–2001

"I still believe in a place called Hope."

 **Democrat**

Activities Law, crosswords, saxophone, welfare reform

Best Freestyler During a crucial 1993 speech to Congress on his health care plan, Clinton's teleprompter was accidentally loaded with the wrong speech. The president, who famously loved to improvise, ad-libbed for ten minutes until the right text could be found.

43

GEORGE W. BUSH

July 6, 1946–

"Dubya"

Term: 2001–2009

"States like these, and their terrorist allies, constitute an axis of evil, arming to threaten the peace of the world."

Republican

Activities Baseball card collecting, clearing brush, tax cuts, the "War on Terror"

Most Understudied The Twenty-Fifth Amendment makes the vice president "acting president" if the president is out of commission. Bush's veep, Dick Cheney, was never president, but he was "acting president" for four hours and twenty minutes total during Bush's term, while the boss was undergoing medical procedures.

RECESS

The pressures of the Oval Office don't leave a whole lot of time for fun, but many presidents have made time for favorite games. Woodrow Wilson played bridge, Warren Harding enjoyed Ping-Pong, Bill Clinton plays Trivial Pursuit, and Barack Obama prefers Scrabble. According to one legend, John Tyler was playing marbles with his sons when he learned that he had just succeeded to the presidency upon William Henry Harrison's death.

Here are a few other presidential ways to pass the time, Junior Geniuses. But remember to line up by the classroom door in fifteen minutes when you hear the bell ring!

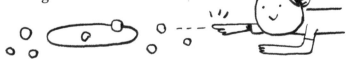

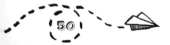

Lame Duck Duck Goose

In politics, a "lame duck" is an officeholder who is still serving out the rest of his or her term even though a replacement has already been elected. Sit in a circle with some friends and play Lame Duck Duck Goose using the names of a president and his eventual replacement. One round could be "Jackson Jackson Van Buren," the next might be "Bush Bush Obama." Once someone in the

circle is tapped with the new name, it's a race between the outgoing president and the incoming president to see who can run around the circle and get to the Oval Office first. It's a fun* way to learn the presidents in order!

*Well, more fun than studying an encyclopedia, anyway.

Grover Cleveland Hangman

When Grover Cleveland was a young sheriff in Buffalo, New York, his duties included manning the gallows when murderers were hanged, making him the only executioner president. So play a round of the word-guessing game Hangman using political names and words. Take turns with a friend being Grover Cleveland. Don't worry about who goes first! You will each get to be Grover Cleveland on two nonconsecutive occasions.

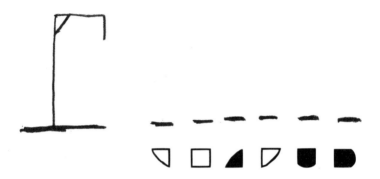

Follow the President

It's like Follow the Leader, but more constitutional! Elect one player president; everyone else is Congress. Everyone has to follow the president's movements and actions, but if half of Congress disagrees with his course, they can vote against it. (No filibustering!) The president can either agree with their suggestion or veto it, in which case Congress needs a two-thirds majority to override it. If this always ends up as a confusing fight and nobody gets to go anywhere—well, that's a valuable lesson about American politics too.

THIRD PERIOD

Before the White House

The youngest person ever to become president *wasn't* John F. Kennedy, as many people believe. JFK was the youngest man ever *elected* president, but Theodore

Roosevelt was almost a full year younger in 1901 when he was sworn in following William McKinley's death. The oldest president ever elected was Ronald Reagan, who was two weeks away from turning seventy at his inauguration. Reagan was asked about the age gap when he ran against the fifty-six-year-old Walter Mondale for reelection. "I will not make age an issue of this campaign," he quipped. "I am not going to exploit, for political purposes, my opponent's youth and inexperience."

On average, the president of the United States has been fifty-four years and eleven months old when he took office. So most of their lives were already behind them when they moved into the White House. They had been soldiers, sailors, teachers, and tailors. In this chapter we're going to travel back in time to when the

presidents of the United States were younger and better looking. In fact, we're going to start when the presidents were *your* age.

Long-Form Birth Certificates

Eight U.S. presidents were born in Virginia—more than any other state. There are two presidents whose birthplaces are still mysterious!

ANDREW JACKSON might have been born in North or South Carolina. The border hadn't been surveyed well at the time, so no one knows.

CHESTER A. ARTHUR said he was born in Vermont, but his rivals claimed he was actually born across the Canadian border in Quebec—which would have made him ineligible for the presidency!

We Are Young

First things first: George Washington never told the truth about cutting down one of his father's prize cherry trees. In fact, he probably never cut down a cherry tree at all. The story first appeared in an 1800 children's biography of Washington by Parson Weems, and most historians believe he made up the story himself to boost sales of his book.

Lincoln's childhood, however, checks out. The "Rail Splitter," as he was called, really did wield an ax from the age of eight, when he helped his family build a new homestead in Indiana. He was the county's champion wrestler, and neighbors claimed they once saw him lift a six-hundred-pound chicken coop. (Okay, that one is probably a Parson Weems–style exaggeration.)

In fact, lots of the presidents were tough little scrappers as kids. As you lazy, modern children sit for hours on a **comfy couch** playing **video games** and sucking sugar from a **juice box**, think about childhoods like these.

James Garfield had the poorest upbringing of any president. (He never heard a piano until he was nineteen years old, and ate his first banana at age twenty-three!) He ran away from home to work on a canal boat, but fell overboard fourteen times in his first six weeks. And he couldn't swim.

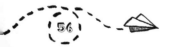

Dwight Eisenhower skinned his knee when he was fifteen, and it got infected. Doctors wanted to amputate it, but Ike refused, and the leg eventually got better.

When **Bill Clinton** was just eight years old, he was mauled by an angry sheep, which knocked him down and butted him ten times.

Andrew Jackson and his brother were taken prisoner by the British during the American Revolution. A British officer ordered Jackson to polish his boots, but young Andy refused. The angry officer sliced the boy's cheek with his sword, and Jackson had a scar there for the rest of his life.

Ulysses S. Grant was such an expert rider as a boy that he could break any horse. When the circus came through town, he could even stay on their trick ponies. One annoyed ringmaster tried to knock Grant off the horse by throwing an angry monkey at him!

But take heart, nerds. A young **Barack Obama** collected Spider-Man and Conan the Barbarian comics, and it didn't keep him from the White House. In fact, even **Teddy Roosevelt** overcame a sickly, asthmatic childhood to become America's manliest president ever.

A Date with Destiny

On July 24, 1963, President Kennedy went out to the White House Rose Garden to meet some boys who had traveled to Washington, D.C., for a Boys Nation convention. One of the boys who shook his hand decided that very day that

he wanted to go into public service. He grew up to be the forty-second U.S. president, Bill Clinton.

On the other hand, railway executive James Roosevelt took his young son Franklin to the White House in 1887 to meet President Grover Cleveland. "My little man," said Cleveland to the young FDR, "I am making a strange wish for you. It is that you may never be president of the United States!" Oops.

The Only President Ever To . . .

 CLIMB THE MATTERHORN? Theodore Roosevelt. (On his honeymoon.)

 EARN HIS EAGLE SCOUT BADGE? Gerald Ford. (He kept the badge his whole life.)

 PATENT AN INVENTION? Abraham Lincoln. (A device to lift riverboats over sandbars.)

 LEAD AN ARCHAEOLOGICAL DIG? Thomas Jefferson. (Indian burial mounds in Virginia.)

 REPORT SEEING A UFO? Jimmy Carter. (In Leary, Georgia, in 1969.)

Eggheads and Dropouts

Most presidents studied hard in school. Woodrow Wilson, who was the president of Princeton University before he went into politics, was the only president with a PhD. Bill Clinton is our only president who was a Rhodes scholar, and George W. Bush is the only president with a master's in business.

But not all presidents got a diploma. In fact, nine of them, including Washington and Lincoln, attended no college at all! Lincoln was a lawyer, but he never went to law school. He spent three years borrowing books from neighbors and studying the law on his own. The least educated president was Lincoln's successor, Andrew Johnson, who never attended a day of school in his life! But don't feel jealous, Junior Geniuses. Johnson was

apprenticed out to a tailor when he was just ten years old. He could barely read and couldn't write at all when he married at eighteen, so his new wife, Eliza, had to teach him letters and numbers.

Being a prankster at school doesn't disqualify you from the presidency. Andrew Jackson, as a boy, used to dig up people's outhouses in the dead of night. Chester A. Arthur dumped his college's bell into the Erie Canal. Even George W. Bush was arrested twice at Yale—once for stealing a Christmas wreath from a hotel lobby!

Working for a Living

The most common job for a budding president-to-be? The law. Twenty-six U.S. presidents, more than half, were lawyers. More than half were also governors.

Extra Credit

William Howard Taft was even governor of the Philippines! (The United States occupied the Philippines for a time after the Spanish-American War.)

But some presidents have more unusual items on their résumés! Warren Harding was a newspaper editor. George W. Bush owned the Texas Rangers—but instead of enjoying the games from a luxury box, he preferred to munch on hot dogs and Cracker Jack in the stands with fans. Lyndon Johnson picked grapes, fixed cars, and even taught fifth grade before lucking into politics.

Here are five more not-very-presidential professions.

The Peanut Farmer President. Jimmy Carter used the campaign slogan "Not Just Peanuts," because he had inherited his family's peanut farm after leaving the navy.

The Haberdasher President. A haberdashery is a men's clothing store, like the one Harry Truman used to run in Kansas City. The shop failed, but Truman refused to declare bankruptcy, and spent decades slowly paying off every one of his debts.

The Model President. During the 1940s, good-looking Gerald Ford was a fashion model for *Look* and *Cosmopolitan* magazines.

The Fake Sports-Announcer President. Before heading out to Hollywood to become an actor in B movies, Ronald Reagan was a baseball announcer. One of his jobs was to report on Chicago Cubs games—without ever going to the ballpark! He would sit in a radio studio and make up descriptions of the game as updates came in over the telegraph. Once, in 1934, the telegraph

machine broke, and Reagan played for time, improvising an amazingly long series of foul balls until the connection was fixed.

The Batman President. When Teddy Roosevelt was New York's police commissioner, he would often prowl the streets by night in a black cape with his hat pulled down over his eyes, hoping to catch cops who were drunk on duty.

Mister President

Some of the presidents who appear on money today had lots of it. Others had none at all.

Rich Prez

WASHINGTON. Married a wealthy widow. His fortune would be worth $525 million today!

HOOVER. A self-made multimillionaire who struck gold in China and Australia!

KENNEDY. JFK's wealthy father gave each of his kids a million dollars as a twenty-first birthday present!

Poor Prez

FILLMORE. Worked his whole childhood to support nine brothers and sisters. Learned to read from the dictionary.

GRANT. Lost all his savings on his son's banking venture, had to hawk his Civil War souvenirs. Died broke, but his memoir became a bestseller.

JOHNSON. Gave his wife a $2.50 ring from Sears on their wedding day.

Heavy Medals

Franklin Pierce very nearly lost the 1852 presidential election because of his lousy reputation from the Mexican War. He passed out twice in battle, and his men took to calling him "Fainting Frank." But many

Look it Up!

presidents have had more impressive war records. Let's (posthumously) award some made-up citations to these brave presidents-to-be.

The Honorable Order of Gilligan. After the sinking of his torpedo boat, PT-109, in the Pacific during World War II, Lieutenant John F. Kennedy led the survivors to a nearby island, pulling his injured shipmate by holding a life-jacket strap in his teeth. Kennedy later sent for help by carving a message into a coconut, and the coconut sat on the Oval Office desk when he was president.

The Bronze Whiskey Bottle. After General Grant won at Shiloh, the bloodiest engagement in U.S. history up to that time, rumors began to spread that he'd been drunk at the battle. "Then find out what kind of whiskey he drinks," Lincoln is said to have replied, "and send a barrel to my other generals."

The Outstanding Combat in Peacetime Award. Andrew Jackson's defense of New Orleans in 1815 was one of the most important American victories of the War of 1812. There's only one problem: The war was already over! The peace treaty with the British had been signed more than two weeks earlier, but word hadn't yet reached Louisiana.

The Purple Retina. Harry Truman badly wanted to enlist in World War I, but he knew his eyesight wasn't good enough. In the end, he passed the vision test by memorizing the eye chart in advance!

The Distinguished Service against Jellyfish Award. In 1943 the first President Bush became the youngest pilot in navy history, and went on to fly fifty-eight missions in the Pacific. In 1944, he was shot down during a raid, but completed his bombing run anyway, eventually jumping from his burning plane into the Pacific. He was chased by Japanese boats and stung by jellyfish before being rescued by an American submarine.

The Glue Factory Ribbon. Rutherford B. Hayes was wounded four times in the Civil War, and had no less than four horses shot out from under him!

The Legion of Fast Promotion. Dwight D. Eisenhower, who led Allied forces to victory in World War II, wasn't even a colonel until 1941, the same year America entered the war! His swift promotion ended in 1944, with Ike being made a five-star general after planning for D-day, the largest amphibious landing in world military history.

Peaking Early

Some presidents did their very best work *before* becoming leader of the free world.

YEARS BEFORE THE PRESIDENCY

1   Zachary Taylor wins the Mexican-American War.

2   John Quincy Adams writes the Monroe Doctrine.

3   Ulysses S. Grant wins the Civil War.

11   Herbert Hoover leaves his lucrative businesses to help lead humanitarian efforts in Europe following World War I. His efforts helped feed 300 million people with 46 million tons of food!

20   James Madison drafts the Bill of Rights.

24   Thomas Jefferson writes the Declaration of Independence.

27   Ronald Reagan stars opposite a chimp in *Bedtime for Bonzo*.

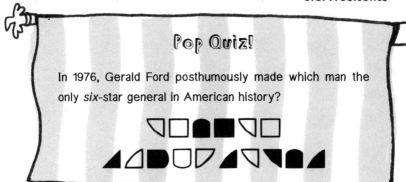

Pop Quiz!

In 1976, Gerald Ford posthumously made which man the only *six*-star general in American history?

No Campaign, No Gain

To serve as president, you have to run for president. (Or, in eight cases, run for vice president, and then have the president die.)

Extra Credit

Alternately, you could be Gerald Ford, our only president never elected to *either* office! He was appointed VP to replace Spiro Agnew, who resigned, and then Ford became president when Nixon resigned.

In the early days of the republic, presidential elections were a little bit screwy. Presidential candidates didn't choose running mates back then. Instead, the second-place candidate—today we would call him "the loser"—became vice president. So the president and his veep were likely to be political opponents! (This first happened to John Adams and Thomas Jefferson in 1796.)

Even weirder, the popular vote didn't matter! Until about 1824, most of the presidential electors in the electoral college were chosen by state legislatures, not statewide votes.

But even today, with almost sixty presidential elections under America's belt, things can sometimes get . . . a little weird. Here are five elections that make all the Bush/Gore nuttiness in 2000 look downright boring.

1876! Hayes Beats Tilden But Not Really.

Four states returned hotly contested election results that year, with Samuel Tilden clearly winning the popular vote. But a backroom deal delivered all four disputed states to Rutherford B. Hayes, who took the oath of office in secret for fear of a coup by Tilden supporters. Hayes was called "His Fraudulency" for the rest of his presidency.

1912! Wilson Beats Two Other Presidents.

William Howard Taft set a record for unpopularity by finishing *third* to two other presidents: Woodrow Wilson and Theodore Roosevelt (who

ran as a third-party candidate). "I am glad to be going," Taft said with a shrug. "I have one consolation: No one candidate was ever elected ex-president by such a large majority!"

1948! Dewey ~~Beats~~ Truman. Harry Truman came from behind in the last month of the campaign with a whirlwind 31,000-mile tour of the country, during which he gave 356 speeches. Everyone was so sure Truman's opponent Thomas Dewey would win that the *Chicago Tribune* even ran a "Dewey Defeats Truman" front page story the next day. Instead, Truman won easily, and was photographed grinning at the mistaken headline.

1820! Monroe Beats . . . Um, Nobody.
During a prosperous time called the Era of Good Feelings, James Monroe won reelection unopposed. A single New Hampshire elector cast a dissenting vote, perhaps so that George Washington would continue to be the only president ever elected unanimously.

Unsound Bites

The very first election slogan in American history is still one of the catchiest: "Tippecanoe and Tyler Too," for William Henry Harrison, hero of the Battle of Tippecanoe, and his running mate, John Tyler. Despite Harrison's account of events, Tippecanoe was actually closer to a bloody draw than a tactical success.

Harrison also campaigned using an image of a log cabin, and painted his opponent, Martin Van Buren, as an out-of-touch aristocrat. That was pretty rich, since Harrison lived in a twenty-two-room mansion, while Van Buren had risen from poverty!

ART CLASS

William Henry Harrison may not have been born in a log cabin, but seven other presidents were.

ANDREW JACKSON

ZACHARY TAYLOR

MILLARD FILLMORE

JAMES BUCHANAN

JAMES GARFIELD

ABRAHAM LINCOLN

ULYSSES S. GRANT

Being raised in a log cabin meant a rugged frontier upbringing, which really paid off at the polls. In fact, no president was born in a hospital until our thirty-ninth president, Jimmy Carter! The first thirty-eight were all born at home.

Would you like to be president someday, Junior Geniuses? I assume you didn't have a log-cabin childhood, but I can help with that. Today we're going to make our *own* log cabins. You'll need a few things:

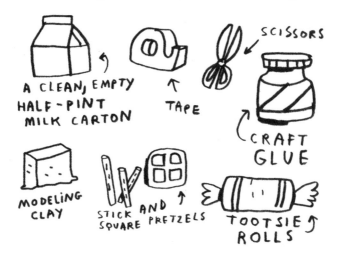

A CLEAN, EMPTY HALF-PINT MILK CARTON

TAPE

SCISSORS

CRAFT GLUE

MODELING CLAY

STICK AND SQUARE PRETZELS

TOOTSIE ROLLS

MILK

First, cut off the top flap of the carton, so the top looks more like a roof. Unfortunately, the glue on that flap was what held the top of the carton together, so apply Scotch tape along the roofline.

Now it's time to put the logs on your cabin. Squirt a generous layer of craft glue onto one face of the cartoon, and using a pretzel, smear it into an even coating. (School

glue will work too, but it's runnier and takes longer to dry, so it's harder to work with.) Starting at the bottom, press pretzels horizontally into the glue. If you don't like the two hollow triangles at the top of the carton, fill them with modeling clay and press pretzels into the clay.

For Experts Only!

After the "logs" are on, use those little square pretzels to give your cabin some doors or windows. Glue on a stack of Tootsie Rolls for a chimney.

Repeat the log gluing for the other five faces of the carton, and *ta-da*! Your cabin is complete and you are ready for a miserable, hardscrabble childhood in the backwoods of Kentucky or Ohio. See you in the Oval Office in forty years, Mr. or Madam President!

FOURTH PERIOD

Riding the Tiger

People run themselves ragged trying to be president, but sometimes, when they get there, they find the job is even harder than they ever imagined. John Quincy Adams called his term in office "the four most miserable years of my life." Bill Clinton compared it to running a cemetery: "You've got a lot of people under you, and nobody's listening." Harry Truman summed it up best: "Being a president is like riding a tiger."

The only problem with learning about the accomplishments of historical presidents is that *it can be super-boring*, what with all the "tariffs" and the "civil service reform" and whatnot. Rutherford B. Hayes supported the gold standard?!? Hold on a second while I . . .

Oops, sorry! I nodded off for a second.

It doesn't have to be that way, Junior Geniuses! This period, we're going to look at the highlights of more than two centuries of presidencies—but with the boring parts removed! Let's start where every presidential term starts: Inauguration Day.

Meet the New Boss

Abraham Lincoln's promise to govern "with malice toward none, with charity toward all." FDR's reminder that "the only thing we have to fear is fear itself."

Kennedy's admonition to "ask not what your country can do for you—ask what you can do for your country." All these pivotal moments in American history happened at presidential inaugurations.

But George Washington almost missed the very first Inauguration Day—he was short on cash at the time, and a friend had to loan him six hundred dollars so he could make the journey. (Martha stayed home.)

Extra Credit

Inaugurations were simple back then—there wasn't even a parade until 1805, when Thomas Jefferson got on his horse to ride back to the White House, and a bunch of onlookers decided to follow him home!

Look IT UP!

Today, of course, the inauguration is a big quadrennial party in Washington, and nobody wants to go to a lame party. Here are some party-planning tips that presidential history has taught us.

Clean up first! A historic blizzard hit D.C. the day before John F. Kennedy's inauguration. The army used flamethrowers to melt away the snowdrifts.

Don't forget decorations! When George Washington rode into Philadelphia for his swearing-in, he got a special surprise: The artist Charles Willson Peale had built an arch that would lower a laurel wreath onto Washington's head as he rode under it. Fancy!

Stock up on snacks! After Thomas Jefferson was sworn in, he returned to the boardinghouse near the Capitol where he'd been staying. Every place at the dining table was taken, so the new president went to bed hungry.

No party crashers! Just over a year before he shot Abraham Lincoln, John Wilkes Booth actually attended Abe's second inauguration and is visible in photos of the event!

Make it casual! James Earl Carter Jr. is our only president ever inaugurated using a nickname. He was sworn in as "Jimmy."

Easy on the punch! Andrew Johnson, battling typhoid fever in 1861, tried to self-medicate with whiskey, and gave a drunken, rambling speech at his inauguration. Some called for his impeachment, but Lincoln stood by his veep, saying, "It has been a severe lesson for Andy, but I do not think he will do it again."

Don't bore your guests! William Henry Harrison gave the longest inaugural speech in history: 8,443 words in two hours. In a snowstorm. Without his hat and overcoat. He caught a chill and was dead of pneumonia a month later, never having signed a single bill as president. Harrison was the only president who studied to be a doctor—he should have known better!

Keep it down! Crowds of Andrew Jackson's, um, *less refined* supporters from out West packed into his White House party, breaking thousands of dollars in china and spitting tobacco juice everywhere. Jackson himself snuck out a window and had to spend the night at a tavern!

Four Snores and Seven Years Ago . . .

When Zachary Taylor took office in 1849, Inauguration Day fell on a Sunday, so the oath wasn't given until the following morning. But wait. If James K. Polk's term had ended, but Taylor hadn't been sworn in yet, who was president all day Sunday? Senator David Rice Atchison of Kansas was the president pro tempore of the Senate at the time, theoretically next in the line of succession, so he spent the rest of his life claiming that he had actually been the twelfth president of the United States, for about twenty-four hours. Almost all of which, by the way, he spent sound asleep! "That was the honestest administration this country ever had," Atchison liked to joke.

Where the Magic Happens

Many people spend their whole lives trying to work their way up to a fancy corner office. But the most powerful person on Earth has a cornerless office! There's a long tradition of presidents using oval-shaped rooms to conduct business. George Washington remodeled his presidential mansion by adding a special room with a set of rounded bow windows where he could receive visitors, and this design carried over to the White House. But many of his successors just worked out of the Residence part of the White House. Lincoln signed the Emancipation Proclamation in the room we today call the Lincoln Bedroom, for example.

President Taft was the first Chief Executive to work out of an Oval Office in the White House's West Wing. Today's Oval Office dates back to 1934, when FDR and his architects renovated the West Wing and created a new, larger presidential office. It hasn't changed much since then, though most presidents choose to redecorate with new drapes and furniture. Let's take a tour of what might be the most famous room in the world.

A. Presidential seal on carpet

B. Grandfather clock, built in Boston around 1800

C. Presidents get to choose their own art

D. Fireplace, backdrop for many a photo op

E. Nixon's hidden recording devices

F. The marble mantel, with Swedish ivy that has outlasted ten presidents!

 G. Presidents always used a phone booth in the hall until 1929, when Herbert Hoover finally had a phone installed on the desk

H. The *Resolute* desk, an 1880 gift from Queen Victoria, was built from the timbers of the HMS *Resolute*, an Arctic exploration ship

I. This panel was added to hide FDR's knee braces—when Kennedy's kids played under the desk, it became the door of their "house"

J. Reagan kept a bag of Camp David acorns on the desk, to feed White House squirrels. When the Bushes moved in with their spaniel Millie, Reagan left the squirrels a note: "Beware of the dog!"

K. Truman's famous THE BUCK STOP HERE sign rested . . . well, here

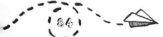

L. For his desk chair, LBJ used a vinyl helicopter seat, complete with ashtray and flotation cushion!

M. LBJ also had added these four buttons on the desk for when he got thirsty. Mmm . . . Fresca.

N. An original cast of Frederic Remington's famous statue *The Bronco Buster*

O. Two flags: the U.S. flag and the presidential flag

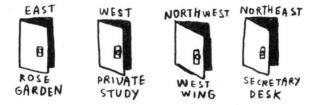

P. (East door) Door to the Rose Garden

Q. (West door) Hidden door to president's private study— Clinton used to nap here

R. (Northwest door) Door to the West Wing

S. (Northeast door) Door to the office of the president's secretary

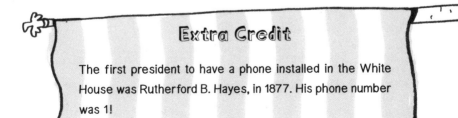

Extra Credit

The first president to have a phone installed in the White House was Rutherford B. Hayes, in 1877. His phone number was 1!

Executive Action

Many presidents are military heroes *before* they enter politics, and once they get to the White House, they spend their days on boring stuff like cabinet meetings and press conferences. But here are a few exciting exceptions.

George Washington is . . . THE ENFORCER!

In 1794, a Pennsylvania farm protest against a new whiskey tax was threatening to turn into an armed rebellion. President Washington himself put on his old uniform and rode out at the head of an army to put down the revolt, which quickly collapsed.

James Madison is . . . THE DEFENDER!

During the War of 1812, British forces moved south from Canada, occupied Washington, D.C., and set the capital

on fire. President Madison himself had been leading a U.S. militia at the nearby Battle of Bladensburg and was very nearly captured! Canadians still fondly remember this as "the time we burned down your White House."

Andrew Jackson is . . . THE PUNISHER!

The first assassination attempt in presidential history happened in 1835, when Richard Lawrence, an insane housepainter claiming to be the king of England, came at Andrew Jackson with two pistols. When both guns misfired (a 1 in 125,000 chance!), the president responded by whacking the would-be assassin with his cane.

Theodore Roosevelt is . . . THE INTIMIDATOR!

Teddy lined the White House basement with judo mats so he could tussle with aides and even visiting dignitaries. In 1909, he received letters from army cavalrymen complaining at having to ride twenty-five miles a day. The fifty-one-year-old president hopped on his horse and rode *one hundred* miles in one day, just to shame the troops. That shut them up!

Thank You Notes

Once they take office, presidents are always surprised by how hard it is to actually get anything done. But many administrations really did change the country—or even the world—forever. Here's a list of some historic presidential contributions, so you know who to thank.

Every Time You . . .	You Can Thank . . .
Eat Thanksgiving leftovers	Abraham Lincoln, who made Thanksgiving a national holiday in response to a letter from Sarah Josepha Hale—the same woman who wrote "Mary Had a Little Lamb."
Check the time	Chester Arthur, who organized the conference that established the prime meridian through London and led to today's standard time zones.
Buy cheap clothing and toys	Richard Nixon, who opened trade relations with China in 1972.
Visit a national park	Ulysses Grant, who created the world's first national park, Yellowstone, in 1872.
Eat something and don't die	Theodore Roosevelt, who signed the Pure Food and Drug Act, making American food safer and less gross.
Don't have to work in a factory all day	Woodrow Wilson, who created the eight-hour workday and banned child labor in America.

Use the freeway	**Dwight Eisenhower**, who created the Interstate Highway System. The project used enough cement to build six sidewalks to the moon!
Say "okay"	**Martin Van Buren**, who helped popularize "O.K." (meaning "oll korrect" or "all correct") in his 1840 campaign, since it could also stand for his nickname, "Old Kinderhook."
Recite the Pledge of Allegiance	**Benjamin Harrison**, who called on schoolkids to try a new flag ceremony on October 12, 1892, to celebrate the four hundredth anniversary of Columbus's landing. Little did he know we'd still be doing it over a century later!
Go anywhere west of Illinois	**Thomas Jefferson**, who doubled the size of the nation by buying the Louisiana Purchase from France—at less than three cents an acre! What a deal.

Extra Credit

Thomas Jefferson also sent the Lewis and Clark Expedition into the newly purchased Louisiana Territory. He speculated that they might find woolly mammoths, active volcanoes, and mountains made of salt! But Jefferson's science actually seems solid compared to John Quincy Adams's, who thought the earth might be hollow, and planned to send an expedition to the North Pole in hopes of finding an opening to the interior! (Sadly, he was voted out of office before this crazy-sauce plan could come together.)

The Quotable President

Even in our highly scripted television age, presidents still blow their lines from time to time. Here are my favorite nationally reported goofs from the past half century of presidents.

Richard Nixon

"I was not lying. I said things that later on seemed to be untrue."

Gerald Ford

"Things are more like they are now than they have ever been."

Jimmy Carter

"I hope that history will present me with maybe two words. One is peace. The other is human rights."

Ronald Reagan

"We are trying to get unemployment to go up, and I think we're going to succeed."

George H. W. Bush

"I have opinions of my own—strong opinions—but I don't always agree with them."

Bill Clinton

"This is still the greatest country in the world, if we just steel our wills and lose our minds."

"If you're a single mother with two children . . . you're workin' hard to put food on your family."

George W. Bush

"The Middle East is obviously an issue that has plagued the region for centuries."

Barack Obama

Pop Quiz!

Can you complete this famous quote from a 1961 John F. Kennedy speech to Congress? "I believe that this nation should commit itself to achieving the goal, before this decade is out, of landing a _____ and returning him safely to the Earth."

The Obscurity Council

Even presidents with problematic legacies have *some* bright spots on their résumés. You're not a fan of Nixon? Well, he signed the first Clean Air Act and Clean

Water Act. Whatever you think of Jimmy Carter, he brokered a peace accord between Israel and Egypt. Whatever you think of George W. Bush,

he tripled U.S. aid to Africa, preventing over a million deaths from AIDS alone.

But what about the presidents nobody even remembers, the ones you'll never see on Mount Rushmore or on paper money? Some of these little-known presidents with weird facial hair actually did a pretty solid job.

WHO THE HECK IS . . . **James K. Polk?** Polk's nomination was the first bit of news ever reported via telegraph, and listeners were so surprised that they assumed the new invention must

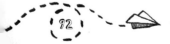

be broken! But despite his anonymity, he achieved all his campaign promises in just one term, and quit! But the poor guy worked himself literally to death in the White House. He hardly ever took a day off, and died suddenly just three months after leaving office.

WHO THE HECK IS . . . Chester A. Arthur? Chester Alan Arthur was our only president never to serve in a high government *or* military office before running on a presidential ticket. But when he succeeded the assassinated James Garfield, he surprised everyone by actually being a pretty good president. The veep who nobody liked or trusted left office as one of the most respected men in America.

WHO THE HECK IS . . . Harry S. Truman? When FDR died in 1945, his vice president, Harry Truman, had met with him only *twice*. But Truman went on to become one of the most influential modern presidents, expanding the New Deal, containing the Soviet Union, rebuilding postwar Europe, and desegregating the military. Not bad for a failed shopkeeper from Missouri.

Haters Gonna Hate

No president is without his critics. Even Lincoln was dissed all the time, with papers calling him a "clown," a "rube," and an "ugly baboon." After he delivered the Gettysburg Address, one of the finest speeches in world history, the *Chicago Times* wrote, "The cheeks of every American must tingle with shame as he reads [these] silly, flat, and dish-watery utterances."

SPEAKING OF FLAT, DISHWATERY THINGS, LET'S GO TO THE CAFETERIA FOR LUNCH!

LUNCH

I'm afraid presidents can be picky eaters, Junior Geniuses. Bush 41 hated broccoli. Reagan's favorite food was jelly beans.

But why did so many presidents fill up on so many weird foods? Grant's favorite breakfast was cucumbers soaked in vinegar, while Nixon put ketchup in his cottage cheese. Buchanan threw sauerkraut-and-mashed-potato parties, and George H. W. Bush snacked on pork rinds with Tabasco sauce. Maybe the most controversial presidential food policy is Barack Obama's: He doesn't really like ice cream! (He blames an unpleasant job behind an ice-cream counter as a teenager.)

Still, it's easy to see why many presidents come into office Obama-trim and leave looking more like a Cleveland or a Taft. *There's food everywhere:* state dinners, White House luncheons, a kitchen that never closes. Even staffers have unlimited access to free soda and, after 5 p.m., free French fries. (On Fridays, there's also free frozen yogurt with crushed Oreos.)

Junior Genius Joviality

Q: Who was the only orange-flavored U.S. president?

A: Sherbet Hoover.

Thomas Jefferson himself may have introduced French fries to America—at a White House dinner in 1802, "potatoes served in the French manner" were on the menu. He's also credited with popularizing waffles in this country, bringing a waffle iron with him when he moved back from France! With that in mind, here's

a breakfast recipe to help you bring forth on your countertop a new preparation, conceived in delectability, and dedicated to the proposition that not all men are decorated equal.

George Waffleton, Thomas Jellyson, and Abraham Linkin'

waffles
blueberries or chocolate chips (for eyes)
wafer cookies, bananas, or peanut butter (for noses)
strawberries or bacon (for mouths)
whipped cream
strawberry jam
sausage links

Directions

1. You'll need three waffles if you're going to make all three presidents. Either make them from scratch from a favorite recipe (and with grown-up help) or use frozen toaster waffles. Round waffles are better but square ones will work.

2. All three presidents will need faces made from your favorite toppings. I've listed some suggestions above,

but the only "checks and balances" here are your own creativity. For eyes, stick blueberries or chocolate chips into the appropriate little square waffle holes. A diagonally sliced banana, a cookie, or a blob of peanut butter could become a nose. A thin strip of strawberry or bacon might be a mouth.

BLUEBERRIES
CHOCOLATE CHIPS
SYRUP
COOKIE STRAWBERRY
BACON
BANANA

MISTER PRESIDENT, ARE YOU WAFFLING ON THIS ISSUE?

3. After you've "elected" the faces you like, it's time to style the presidents with their famous hair. Squirt some whipped cream on either side of the waffle to give George Waffleton his distinctive do. Thomas Jellyson gets the same

HAIR TO THE CHIEF!

haircut, but this time use strawberry jam—after all, the "Father of the Declaration of Independence and Also Waffles" *was* our first red-headed president. Abraham Linkin's beard and maybe his eyebrows are made of warmed-up sausage links. (He could have a stovepipe hat made out of bacon as well.)

4. Serve to friends with a bottle of Log Cabin syrup. You might have to "rush more" waffles out to the table if they demand a second term!

IN BACON WE TRUST!

5. Maybe don't use that hilarious "rush more" joke with your friends, though, because what if they laugh so hard they choke on their waffles?

FIFTH PERIOD

All the Presidents as Men

Let's face it, Junior Geniuses: When Americans think about their presidents, we probably don't think about their policy achievements first. Instead we think about their public personas: Jefferson being all smart and whatnot, Lincoln being folksy and tall, Clinton stuffing his face with Big Macs, Bush mangling the English language. In this chapter, we're going to look at the personal feats and foibles of the men *behind* the podium with a bald eagle on it.

Photo Ops

Let's be honest: Looks matter in politics. When Richard
Nixon debated John F. Kennedy in the 1960 campaign,
radio listeners thought Nixon won the debate. But TV
viewers could see that Kennedy was handsome, while
Nixon looked sweaty and unshaven, and they called the
debate for Kennedy. Nixon's mom was so concerned by
his appearance that she even called him after the debate
to see if he was okay!

But in the days before TV, many weird-looking presidents made it to the White House.
James Buchanan was nearsighted
in one eye and farsighted in the
other, so he always tipped his
head oddly when talking to people.

HMMM

Lincoln was considered so ugly that he even joked about it. When a newspaper called him "two-faced," Lincoln replied, "If I were two-faced, would I be wearing this one?"

Lincoln was actually clean-shaven until 1860, when an eleven-year-old girl named Grace Bedell wrote him a letter suggesting he grow a beard.

YOU WOULD LOOK A GREAT DEAL BETTER FOR YOUR FACE IS SO THIN. ALL THE LADIES LIKE WHISKERS AND THEY WOULD TEASE THEIR HUSBANDS TO VOTE FOR YOU AND THEN YOU WOULD BE PRESIDENT.

But Lincoln (and little Grace) started a trend. Eight of the next ten presidents had facial hair. Ever since the electric razor was invented, however, every U.S. president has been clean-shaven.

Here are more classic presidential haircuts that are hard to imagine on a modern commander in chief.

POLK
THE MULLET

HAYES
THE DUMBLEDORE

ARTHUR
THE MUTTON CHOPS

HARRISON
THE SANTA CLAUS

TAFT
THE HANDLEBAR

EISENHOWER
THE CUE BALL

The Tall and the Short of It

Not all presidents are the same size.

TALLEST Abraham Lincoln: 6'4". (Without the hat, that is. When asked his height, Lincoln would respond, "Tall enough to reach the ground!")

HEAVIEST William Howard Taft: 340 lbs. (He once got stuck in the White House bathtub and had to have a larger one installed.)

SHORTEST AND LIGHTEST James Madison: 5'3", 100 lbs. (Washington Irving called him a "withered little apple-john")

MOST TENTACLES President Kang from *The Simpsons*. (Note: not a real president.)

The Bright House

Maybe a few American presidents would have been Junior Geniuses like you, if they had applied themselves and made it through the rigorous selection process. Which of these brainy presidents would you nominate as posthumous Junior Geniuses?

☐ **Thomas Jefferson.** Used to get up at 5 a.m. every morning to study science.

☐ **John Quincy Adams.** Spoke eight languages, more than any other president.

☐ **Franklin Pierce.** Memorized his entire 3,319-word inaugural address.

☐ **James Garfield.** Could write in Greek with his left hand and Latin with his right . . . . at the same time!

☐ **Theodore Roosevelt.** Read a book a day in the White House before breakfast.

☐ **Harry Truman.** Had read every book in his hometown library by age fifteen.

☐ **Jimmy Carter.** Could speed-read more than two thousand words a minute.

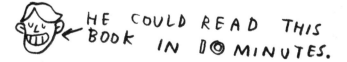
HE COULD READ THIS BOOK IN 10 MINUTES.

Name Recognition

Do you know who Leslie King and William Blythe are? Each boy adopted his stepfather's name when he was young. We know them better as Gerald Ford and Bill Clinton, respectively.

In fact, several U.S. presidents rose to fame under an assumed name—their middle name, in fact.

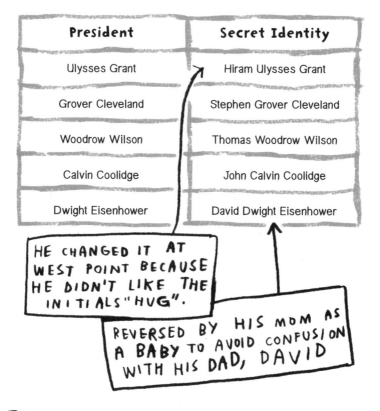

President	Secret Identity
Ulysses Grant	Hiram Ulysses Grant
Grover Cleveland	Stephen Grover Cleveland
Woodrow Wilson	Thomas Woodrow Wilson
Calvin Coolidge	John Calvin Coolidge
Dwight Eisenhower	David Dwight Eisenhower

HE CHANGED IT AT WEST POINT BECAUSE HE DIDN'T LIKE THE INITIALS "HUG".

REVERSED BY HIS MOM AS A BABY TO AVOID CONFUSION WITH HIS DAD, DAVID

Two U.S. presidents had another president's last name for a middle name: Ronald *Wilson* Reagan and William *Jefferson* Clinton. But the oddest presidential middle name was Harry S. Truman's. His *S* stood for . . . nothing, just *S*! It was a compromise choice to honor his two grandpas, named Solomon and Shipp.

Homework

There have been six chief executives named James, making it the most popular presidential first name. How many can you think of?

7 Ways to Dress Like a President!

Today, every president dresses pretty much the same: dark suit, power tie, flag pin. But presidential style can be whatever you want it to be—because power is *fabulous*!

SPLURGE! Chester Arthur was a clotheshorse who owned more than eighty pairs of pants. When he was nominated as vice president, he celebrated by going to Brooks Brothers and buying a new $726 wardrobe. That's—hold on to your muttonchops—more than $14,000 in today's money!

GO MODERN! James Madison was the first president to wear pants! (No, Washington, Adams, and Jefferson weren't naked. But they wore knee breeches, not modern trousers.)

DRESS DOWN! Zachary Taylor's troops nicknamed him "Old Rough and Ready" because, even in battle, he preferred an old straw hat and rumpled work clothes to a uniform.

ACCESSORIZE! But be practical. Lincoln used to keep important papers in his famous hat.

DO IT YOURSELF! Andrew Johnson, a former tailor, wore his own handmade suits in office.

TRY VINTAGE! John Quincy Adams hated clothes shopping, and wore the same hat for ten years.

GENDER BEND! When Jimmy Carter was a boy, his family owned a small general store, and the kids would have to use the surplus merchandise. Jimmy's first pair of school shoes was a pair of women's dress shoes that the store had been unable to sell.

Cal on the Carpet

Not every president was a workaholic like James K. Polk. Ulysses Grant and Chester Arthur weren't morning people, and would usually roll into work around ten. Benjamin Harrison liked to knock off around noon! But no president loved his beauty sleep as much as Calvin Coolidge. Coolidge slept up to eleven hours a night, and took an afternoon nap to boot. When he needed to kick back after all this exhausting sleeping, he'd enjoy a cigar on his White House porch rocking chair. When told in 1933 that Coolidge had died, writer Dorothy Parker quipped, "How can they tell?"

Top Sick-ret

On August 10, 1921, at the age of thirty-nine, Franklin Roosevelt enjoyed one of the best days of his life. At his family's summer resort, he sailed, fished, swam, jogged two miles, and even put out a forest fire! The next day he suddenly took ill, and the day after that, he couldn't move his legs. Roosevelt had contracted polio, and never walked more than a few steps at a time for the rest of his life. At the time, sadly, a handicap like that was a huge political no-no, so FDR concealed his illness as much as possible. The Secret Service prevented reporters from photographing the president if his wheelchair or knee braces were visible.

But Roosevelt wasn't the only president with a shocking medical secret.

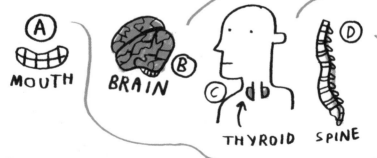

(A) MOUTH

(B) BRAIN

(C) (D) THYROID

SPINE

(A) DIAGNOSIS: MOUTH CANCER. In 1893, Grover Cleveland hopped on a friend's yacht for a "vacation cruise" around Long Island. Actually, he was on board to have a tumor secretly removed 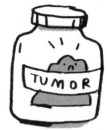 from his upper jaw. Today you can see the tumor in a Philadelphia museum.

(B) DIAGNOSIS: STROKE. Woodrow Wilson suffered a terrible stroke that left him bed bound and half-paralyzed for his last year in office. But nobody found out until after his death! His wife, Edith, limited access to the president and essentially ran the country for all of 1920.

(C) (D) DIAGNOSIS: ADDISON'S DISEASE, HYPO-THYROIDISM, CHRONIC BACK PAIN. President Kennedy liked to project a young, healthy media image to the country, but in reality, he was a mess. For most of his presidency, JFK was in excruciating pain, seeing three different doctors and taking a dozen different medications. As a young man, he was hospitalized dozens of times, and received Catholic last rites on three different occasions.

I Cannot Tell a Lie, Because It Hurts to Talk

Contrary to popular belief, Junior Geniuses, George Washington never used wooden teeth. His dentures were made of much weirder stuff, including gold, lead, donkey teeth, and hippopotamus ivory! They never fit well and always hurt, which is why he looks so tight-lipped and sour in portraits.

Political Players

The presidency is a demanding job, and roughly one president in five hasn't survived it—so keeping fit is important. FDR swam, Nixon bowled, and Bush 43 jogged with his iPod. Herbert Hoover invented a weird, tennis-like game called Hooverball that used a six-pound ball! Oof.

But over the last century or so, the most popular presidential game has been American football. Let's rank five chief executives on their gridiron skills.

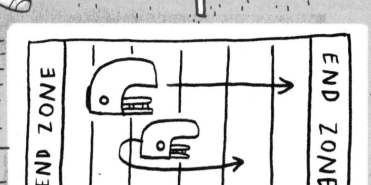

ROOSEVELT. At a time when many wanted to ban college football, Teddy saved the game. He called a White House conference to make the game's rules safer, and thereby created the NCAA.

FORD. A football all-star in college, Ford received NFL offers from the Lions and the Packers. As president, he often took the podium to the University of Michigan fight song instead of "Hail to the Chief."

EISENHOWER. Ike was a good linebacker in college, but he once tried to tackle the great Jim Thorpe and got hurt so badly he had to leave the game.

NIXON. For a 1971 playoff game, Nixon suggested a trick play to Redskins coach George Allen. Washington lost thirteen yards on the play, which ended up being the turning point that cost them the game.

COOLIDGE. In 1925, Coolidge was introduced to the legendary Red Grange "of the Chicago Bears." Not a sports fan, Coolidge said, "Glad to meet you. I always did like animal acts."

Extra Credit

George W. Bush never missed a football game at Yale—because he was the head cheerleader!

Feet of Clay

People are always dedicating statues and elementary schools to ex-presidents, but that doesn't mean they were perfect. Even before modern scandals like Watergate, some administrations were openly corrupt.

James Buchanan's secretary of war embezzled $850,000 in government bonds!

Ulysses Grant's vice president resigned amid the Crédit Mobilier Scandal of 1872.

The Teapot Dome bribery scandal, under Warren Harding, led to two suicides and put a cabinet secretary in jail!

"This is one ~~hell~~ of a job!" complained Harding. **"I have no trouble with my enemies, but my ~~damn~~ friends, they're the ones that keep me walking the floor nights."**

Other presidents had smaller imperfections—but flaws nonetheless. Try not to judge, Junior Geniuses! These men were the products of their time.

George Washington

IN HIS DEFENSE: Won the Revolutionary War.

SECRET SHAME: Currently has $300,000 in New York Public Library fines for two books he checked out in 1789 and never returned. "We're not actively pursuing the overdue fines," a librarian says.

Thomas Jefferson and James Madison

IN THEIR DEFENSE: Wrote the Declaration of Independence and the Constitution.

SECRET SHAME: Rode out into the country in spring 1791 to study plants. Arrested in Vermont for carriage riding on a Sunday.

Andrew Jackson

IN HIS DEFENSE: Only president ever to wipe out the national debt.

SECRET SHAME: Terrible speller. He once tried to sound out "Europe" and ended up writing "Urop."

Benjamin Harrison

IN HIS DEFENSE: Approved the first pensions for disabled veterans.

SECRET SHAME: The worst handshake in White House history. Critics compared it to a "wilted petunia," and aides always hustled him out of the room after speeches, because they knew his wimpy grip would lose him votes.

Herbert Hoover

IN HIS DEFENSE: Donated his entire presidential salary to charity.

SECRET SHAME: Violated Prohibition almost daily. Alcohol was illegal in the U.S. in the 1920s, but it was still allowed on foreign soil. So Hoover just stopped by the Belgian embassy every night for cocktails!

George H. W. Bush

IN HIS DEFENSE: Freed Kuwait in the first Gulf War.

SECRET SHAME: Threw up on the prime minister of Japan at a 1992 banquet. As a result, a new word entered the Japanese language: Bushu-suru, meaning "to barf."

MUSIC CLASS

The president of the United States delighted young voters in 2010 by telling *Rolling Stone* magazine that he had Jay-Z, Nas, and Lil Wayne on the "presidential iPod." But there have been many music lovers in the White House, all the way back to Thomas Jefferson, an accomplished violinist who even owned a priceless Amati, made by the violin maker who trained Stradivari!

I'd certainly rather listen to Jefferson than to Harry Truman (who got up at five every morning to practice the piano) or Warren G. Harding (who played the sousaphone)!

Jimmy Carter even used to type up lists of which pieces of classical music he wanted piped into the White House each day. Be honest: Even if you didn't know that about President Carter, didn't you sort of suspect it?

The most famous track on the presidential play-list, of course, isn't a boring Carter sonata or Bill Clinton's sax solo on *The Arsenio Hall Show*. It's "Hail to the Chief," that brassy fanfare that announces the president's arrival at any gathering. "Hail to the Chief" is actually a show tune—it comes from a London stage adaptation of Walter Scott's epic poem *The Lady of the Lake*. (The "chief" in question is a Scottish chieftain.) It didn't become the default presidential theme song until John Tyler's wife Julia took a shine to it and started requesting it at public events.

Here's a secret about "Hail to the Chief" that almost no one knows, Junior Geniuses: It actually has lyrics! Next time you hear the Marine Band strike up this tune on TV, you can sing along—but I bet you'll be the only one singing!

Hail to the Chief we have chosen
for the nation,
Hail to the Chief! We salute him,
one and all.
Hail to the Chief, as we pledge
cooperation
In proud fulfillment of a great,
noble call.

Yours is the aim to make this grand
country grander,
This you will do, that's our strong,
firm belief.
Hail to the one we selected as
commander,
Hail to the President!
Hail to the Chief!

SIXTH PERIOD

The First Family

Just like you, the president of the United States has a family. And just like your relatives, his relatives are sometimes fun and popular and sometimes *totally embarrassing*. During the Civil War, Mary Todd Lincoln invited her half sister Emily to the White House—even though Emily's husband was a Confederate general! This didn't go over well. Lincoln even had to go in front of Congress to reassure them that his wife wasn't a spy.

More recently, presidents have rolled their eyes at black-sheep brothers like Billy Carter (who used his White House connections to lobby for the Libyans and market his own brand of beer, Billy Beer) and Roger Clinton (such a bozo that his Secret Service nickname was Headache).

But the bad apples are the exceptions in presidential family trees—and a few of these trees have even grown more than one president!

Of course, if you go far enough back, *all* presidents are family. One genealogy database has been able to link George Washington to every U.S. president except Gerald Ford! Barack Obama is George's ninth cousin six times removed.

Mommie Dearest

Sara Roosevelt, FDR's mom, was always very protective of her only son. Perhaps . . . too protective. For one thing, she dressed him like this when he was little.

When little Franklin got married, Sara didn't appreciate the competition. While FDR and Eleanor were on their honeymoon, Sara bought them a house adjoining her own and furnished it to her own tastes!

Mrs. Presidentess

Today, Rutherford B. Hayes's wife, Lucy, might be better remembered than he is. The Hayeses were strictly religious,

and banned cards, billiards, smoking, and drinking from the White House. Instead, the family would sit around the piano every night singing hymns, sometimes with the whole cabinet joining in! *Party!*

As fun as that sounds, there were some complaints about the Hayeses' strict policies, and one White House steward started spiking the punch with rum at parties, to appease annoyed guests. Groups that promoted temperance (the prohibition of alcohol) loved "Lemonade Lucy" and gave the White House a beautiful sideboard in grati-

tude. But there was quite a scandal in 1903 when it was revealed that the sideboard had been sold to a local tavern owner, who gleefully kept it stocked with booze!

Lucy Hayes was also the first presidential wife to be widely referred to as "the first lady"! That's right: The

first nineteen first ladies had no real title. Martha Washington preferred "Lady Washington," while Abigail Adams was called "Mrs. President." John Tyler's wife Julia even insisted on being called "Mrs. Presidentess"!

LADY WASHINGTON

Some first ladies have loved their position—but not Martha Washington, who compared her job to being a "state prisoner." Jane Pierce hated the idea of being first lady so much that, when she heard her husband, Franklin, had been nominated for the presidency, she fainted!

Helen "Nellie" Taft, on the other hand, dreamed of being first lady, and her husband ran for president just to please her. The inauguration was the highlight of her life, but she suffered a stroke just two months after moving into the White House, and never became the hostess she dreamed of being. By all accounts, Taft hated every minute of his term, which probably contributed to the hundred pounds he gained in office.

A Very Special Blossom

Nellie Taft did contribute one important addition to Washington despite her health problems: The famous cherry trees along the Tidal Basin were her pet project. The trees you see today were her second attempt, however. The first two thousand trees imported from Japan were infested with bugs and had to be burned.

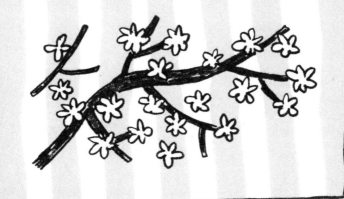

First Legacies

What if there were a Mount Rushmore for first ladies? We all know who the great presidents were, but who were their most influential wives? Here are my suggestions.

Abigail Adams. The 1,200 letters that Mr. and Mrs. Adams wrote each other during their lives reveal that she was every bit his equal when it came to discussing issues and ideas. His letters, by the way, are pretty mushy. He called her "Miss Adorable" and, in one 1762 letter, requisitioned "two or  three million" kisses and "as many hours of [her] company after 9 o'clock" as she could spare. Okay, simmer down there, John Adams.

Dolley Madison. James Madison's wife was an American icon. When she served newfangled "ice cream" at her husband's inaugural ball, it became a national sensation. Every time she adopted a daring new style (turbans, feathers, scarves . . .) even European women copied her. She was also a bona fide action hero! When British troops burned Washington in 1812, they sacked the White House so suddenly that the Madisons' dinner was left sitting on the table, still warm. Mrs. Madison escaped in the nick of time and managed to save a famous portrait of George Washington, which is today the White House's oldest original possession.

Edith Wilson. As we saw last period, Junior Geniuses, Edith Wilson was practically president during the last year of her husband's term. But Edith also gets girl-power bonus points for being a direct descendant of Pocahontas.

Eleanor Roosevelt. The longest-serving first lady was also one of the hardest-working, dedicating herself to an endless series of human rights causes. During one of her first dates with FDR, she insisted her upper-class boyfriend tour a New York City slum with her. As first lady, Eleanor always refused a chauffeur or a Secret Service escort. Instead she carried a pair of pistols to protect herself— one in her glove compartment and one in her handbag.

Extra Credit

There's also plenty of room on Mount Mrs. Rushmore for James Buchanan's wife. He never married and was the only bachelor president.

How I Met Your Mother

What's it like to date a future president? Would he always veto your choice of movie? Here are a few great courtship stories, on a scale of "CUTE" to "CREEPY."

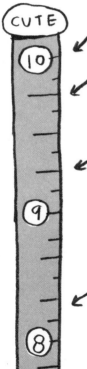

The Trumans. He fell for her in a Sunday school class when they were five.

The Fillmores. They courted by mail for three years! She was teaching, he was law clerking, and they were too poor to visit each other.

The Tylers. They were touring a new naval ship when a gun exploded—killing her father! (Okay, maybe this one is more "epic" than "cute.") She fainted in his arms, and he nursed her back to health after the terrible incident.

The Fords. Gerald Ford was wearing mismatched shoes when he proposed to his wife, Betty.

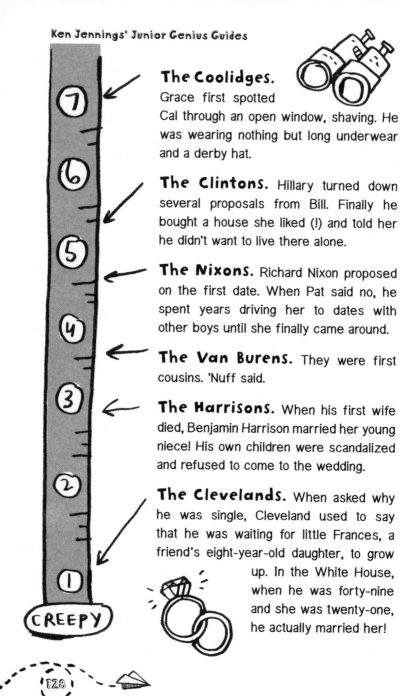

The Coolidges. Grace first spotted Cal through an open window, shaving. He was wearing nothing but long underwear and a derby hat.

The Clintons. Hillary turned down several proposals from Bill. Finally he bought a house she liked (!) and told her he didn't want to live there alone.

The Nixons. Richard Nixon proposed on the first date. When Pat said no, he spent years driving her to dates with other boys until she finally came around.

The Van Burens. They were first cousins. 'Nuff said.

The Harrisons. When his first wife died, Benjamin Harrison married her young niece! His own children were scandalized and refused to come to the wedding.

The Clevelands. When asked why he was single, Cleveland used to say that he was waiting for little Frances, a friend's eight-year-old daughter, to grow up. In the White House, when he was forty-nine and she was twenty-one, he actually married her!

7

6

5

4

3

2

1

CREEPY

Sweet Nothings

More behind-the-scenes glimpses from great presidential romances.

Andrew Johnson's wife, Eliza, was home sick in Tennessee when the Civil War started. She had to cross enemy lines to rejoin her husband!

Ida McKinley sometimes had seizures at dinner parties. The president would cover her head with a napkin and continue the conversation.

Herbert and Lou Hoover both spoke Chinese, which they used to carry on secret conversations at parties.

Dad of the Year

We call Washington the "Father of His Country," but he didn't actually have any children of his own. Maybe that title should really go to John Tyler, who, over the course of two marriages, had *fifteen children*! The tenth president of the United States even has two grandkids that are still alive today!

What's it like to be a kid in the White House? It has its pros and cons.

So much room for activities! Amy Carter had sleepovers in a tree house built in a cedar on the White House's South Lawn.

Playdates with the cabinet. Abe Lincoln's son Tad received a pretend military commission from Secretary of War Edwin Stanton. He proceeded to arm the servants with muskets and even sentenced a doll to death. (Don't worry, his dad commuted the sentence.)

Pranks. Teddy Roosevelt instituted "children's hour" every afternoon at the White House. He and his kids would slide down the White House stairs on cookie sheets, throw

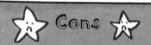

Busy parents. On the other hand, you might miss some of that quality time with Mom and Dad. Barack Obama usually works thirteen- or fourteen-hour days, which doesn't leave a lot of family time. He did make time, however, to read all seven Harry Potter books to his daughter Malia.

No TV. Jackie Kennedy took all the TV sets out of the White House—but eventually had one put back in when her daughter, Caroline, cried about missing *Lassie*.

Secret Service everywhere. Gerald Ford's daughter, Susan, had her high school prom at the White House,

water balloons from the roof, and shoot spitballs at a portrait of Andrew Jackson. Every Roosevelt owned his or her own pair of stilts, which is about the coolest thing I've ever heard of.

Busy parents. If you want to get away with murder, your dad might be too busy to stop you. When told that his daughter was smoking on the White House roof again, Teddy Roosevelt sighed and said, "I can control the nation, or Alice. But not both."

which seems like the least fun prom idea in the history of proms. Jenna Bush's Secret Service agents say she used to try to lose them by driving through red lights!

Your name might be stolen by a candy company. The Curtiss Candy Company claimed that their Baby Ruth candy bar was named for Ruth Cleveland, even though they were clearly trying to cash in on the growing fame of baseball star Babe Ruth.

Pop Quiz!

When future president Zachary Taylor was fighting the Black Hawk War, one of his officers began romancing his daughter Sarah. Taylor tried to end the relationship, but in the end, the two eloped without his consent. The groom later grew up to be an American president himself—but of the Confederacy! What was his name?

Reigning Cats and Dogs

Every president has had pets in the White House—except Millard Fillmore and Chester A. Arthur. (Losers.) (Or maybe allergic.) It's lonely at the top, and pets can provide . . .

Companionship. When Congress was trying to impeach him, Andrew Johnson sought comfort by feeding the White House mice. Warren G. Harding's dog Laddie Boy got his own chair at cabinet meetings and even a dog-biscuit cake.

An image boost. Lucy Hayes's cat Siam, the first Siamese cat in America, was a sensation. Caroline Kennedy's pony Macaroni received thousands of fan letters!

Backing vocals. Thomas Jefferson's mockingbird Dick would sing along to his violin playing.

Milk and wool. Pauline Wayne, the Tafts' dairy cow, was the last cow to live on the White House lawn. During World War I, Woodrow Wilson allowed a flock of sheep to graze there, and their wool was made into Red Cross bandages.

The biggest (and weirdest) menageries belonged to Teddy Roosevelt

and Calvin Coolidge.

The Coolidges were even given an African pygmy hippo with the oddly distinguished name of William Johnson, which they donated to the National Zoo. Today, almost all the pygmy hippos in North American zoos are descended from Mr. Johnson.

Worst White House Pets

4. Teddy Roosevelt's son Quentin used to let his pony Algonquin ride in the White House elevator!

3. Andrew Jackson's parrot, Poll, mimicked her master's bad language. At Jackson's funeral, Poll swore so much she had to be removed from the room.

2. The explorer Zebulon Pike brought Thomas Jefferson two grizzly bears, which lived for a time in cages on the White House lawn!

1. The Marquis de Lafayette gave John Quincy Adams an alligator, which he kept in the East Room bathtub!

Worst White House Pet Names

4. Jimmy Carter's cat Misty Malarky Ying Yang.

3. George Washington's hound Sweet Lips.

2. Lyndon Johnson's beagles Him and Her.

1. John Adams's dog Satan.

Extra Credit

George W. Bush once named a cat India. In return, an offended nationalist group in India urged Hindus to start naming dogs George Bush.

SEVENTH PERIOD

The Uncanny Ex-Presidents

Once you've been the leader of the free world for four or eight years, what do you do for a second act? It's a problem. "A man my age has nothing left to do but move to the country and grow big pumpkins," lamented Chester A. Arthur.

Theodore Roosevelt must not have been a pumpkin fan. Upon leaving office, he became a kind of ex-presidential Indiana Jones, traveling the world having adventures. "It was my last chance to be a boy!" he said of his globe-trotting.

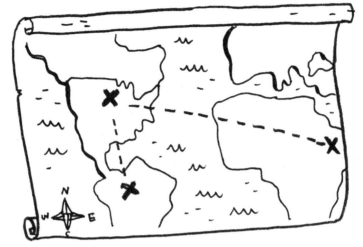

East Africa! Roosevelt and his safari party shoot 512 big-game animals and ship their skins back to the Smithsonian to be mounted. It gets worse, animal lovers: In 1928, Roosevelt's sons go to Indochina and become the first Westerners to track and shoot a giant panda!

St. Louis! Roosevelt becomes the first president to fly in one of the new "aeroplanes." When a pilot offers to take him up, Roosevelt says only, "Thanks!" and hops right into the plane!

The Amazon! Roosevelt leads the first expedition down Brazil's uncharted "River of Doubt," which is today named Rio Roosevelt in his honor.

For Whom the Bell Tolls

But not everyone survived the presidency as robustly as Teddy Roosevelt. In fact, some didn't survive it at all. Being president is one of the most dangerous career choices on the planet. These four all fell to an assassin's bullet.

ABRAHAM LINCOLN

APRIL 14, 1865

Assassin: John Wilkes Booth

Motive: Revenge for the South's defeat in the Civil War

Opportunity: Lincoln was watching a play with his wife at Ford's Theatre, and his bodyguard chose the wrong moment to sneak out for a beer.

Ironic Twist: Less than a year before the assassination, Booth's brother Edwin (also a famous actor) had saved the life of Lincoln's son Robert on a train platform. In later years, Robert was also present at the sites of James Garfield's and William McKinley's assassinations! He was so shaken by the coincidence that he avoided presidential functions for the rest of his life.

Assassin: Charles Guiteau

Motive: Guiteau was a nut who believed Garfield owed him an ambassadorship to France.

Opportunity: Garfield was in the waiting room of a Washington railway station, about to hop on a train.

Ironic Twist: Doctors couldn't find the second bullet, so they spent months poking at Garfield with dirty instruments. Alexander Graham Bell was brought in to try out a newly invented metal detector, but failed. (We now know that the metal bedsprings in Garfield's mattress confused the machine.) The president finally died months later, not from the gunshot but from the subsequent infection.

Assassin: Leon Czolgosz ("CHOAL-gosh")

Motive: Czolgosz was an anarchist—he believed all governments and leaders oppressed their people.

Opportunity: McKinley was shaking hands at the Pan-American Exposition in Buffalo, New York. He usually wore a red carnation as a good luck charm, but had given it away to a young girl just moments before Czolgosz approached.

Ironic Twist: McKinley's first order after being shot was to stop the crowd from beating up his assassin! The president died a week later when doctors couldn't find the fatal bullet.

138

On display nearby at the fair where McKinley had been shot was a newfangled invention that might have saved his life: one of the very first X-ray machines.

JOHN F. KENNEDY NOV. 22, 1963

Assassin: Lee Harvey Oswald

Motive: Unknown. Oswald was killed in police custody (by Dallas nightclub owner Jack Ruby) before he could face trial.

Opportunity: Kennedy was visiting Dallas, and his motorcade route had been published in the local paper. Oswald was at the window of a nearby schoolbook depository.

Ironic Twist: The last thing JFK heard before he was shot was the governor's wife saying, "Mr. President, you can't say Dallas doesn't love you!" Two great British authors died the same day as Kennedy: Aldous Huxley (*Brave New World*) and C. S. Lewis (*The Chronicles of Narnia*). Their deaths went virtually unnoticed due to the assassination.

LEWIS   HUXLEY

Close Calls

At least fifteen other presidents have *survived* assassination attempts. Teddy Roosevelt was shot at a political rally in 1912, three years after he left office. The bullet would have killed him, but it hit a metal glasses case in his pocket, saving his life. Roosevelt showed the crowd his bloody shirt but finished his speech, speaking for ninety more minutes! When Ronald Reagan survived an assassination attempt in 1981, he joked with his surgeons, removing his oxygen mask to tell them, "I hope you are all Republicans!"

Don't Call It a Comeback

On rare occasions, presidents actually find their true calling *after* the voters are tired of them. William Howard Taft, for example, was never happy in the White House, but eight years later, Warren G. Harding nominated him to his dream job: chief justice of the United States.

NOW, IT SAYS ON YOUR RÉSUMÉ YOU WERE THE 27th PRESIDENT?

MHMMM

Finally, Taft was content. "I don't remember that I was ever president," he said happily. He even swore in two presidents, Calvin Coolidge and Herbert Hoover.

Or take these two not-exactly-beloved one-termers: John Quincy Adams and Jimmy Carter. Carter became a tireless activist after leaving the White House, championing low-income housing and spearheading the effort

to wipe out the guinea worm, a tiny parasite that infected 21 *million* people in 1986. Today, that number is down to just 391 people. Someday soon it will be only the second disease ever 100 percent cured by man, after smallpox.

John Quincy Adams was elected to the House of Representatives after leaving the White House and served for seventeen years, becoming a much more popular congressman than he had ever been a president! He pushed for the building of the Smithsonian Institution, and helped free the thirty-six slaves who had escaped their chains and taken over the slave ship *Amistad*. In 1848, he was speaking on the floor of the House when he suffered a massive stroke and died.

Awkward!

In 1868, the U.S. Senate tried to impeach President Andrew Johnson for his moderate policies on post–Civil War Reconstruction. Senator Benjamin Wade would have succeeded Johnson as president, and was already choosing his cabinet . . . but Johnson managed to escape impeachment by one vote. In 1875, Johnson became the only U.S. president elected to the Senate, where he served alongside many of the same men who had tried to impeach him seven years earlier!

On the other hand, we have the presidents who probably *should* have stuck with pumpkin farming. Former president John Tyler, a native Virginian, joined the Confederate government during the Civil War. He was such a political outlaw that he even named his estate Sherwood Forest. When Tyler died in 1862, Lincoln ignored the ex-president's death, the only time this has happened in U.S. history.

Millard Fillmore joined an anti-Catholic, anti-immigrant political movement after he left office, and even ran for president in 1856 for the worst-named third party in history: the Know-Nothings.

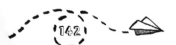

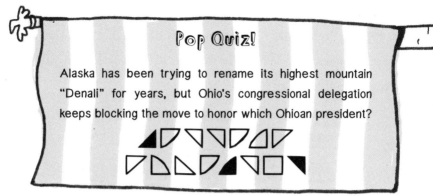

Pop Quiz!

Alaska has been trying to rename its highest mountain "Denali" for years, but Ohio's congressional delegation keeps blocking the move to honor which Ohioan president?

In Da Club

There have been a few times in U.S. history when *no* ex-presidents were alive to look over the new guy's shoulder. Most recently, when Richard Nixon resigned in 1974, *all* his predecessors were dead!

But it's much more common for a whole peanut gallery of ex–chief executives to be alive at one time. At Dwight Eisenhower's inauguration, Herbert Hoover suggested to Harry Truman that they form a "former presidents club," and Truman quickly agreed.

The Presidents Club sometimes has as many as five active members. When George W. Bush was sworn in, these predecessors were all still alive:

GERALD FORD
JIMMY CARTER
BILL CLINTON
RONALD REAGAN
GEORGE H.W. BUSH

Members of the Presidents Club may have been fierce political rivals when they were in office, but in retirement, things are friendlier. LBJ told Nixon about his secret Oval Office recording system, while Ronald Reagan taught Bill Clinton how to give a crisper salute.

Clinton and George H. W. Bush needled each other constantly during their 1992 race for the White House, but in retirement, they're pretty much besties. The two have teamed up to raise money for victims of the 2004 Indian Ocean tsunami and Hurricane Katrina. Bush's kids even call Clinton their "brother from another mother."

BILL C. + GEORGE B. BFF!
2 COOL
SO AWESOMEZ
WE RULE

Homework

Next time a grown-up jokes that they're too old and tired to play with you, Junior Geniuses, remind them how George H. W. Bush celebrated his eightieth and eighty-fifth birthdays—by skydiving from thirteen thousand feet!

Grumpy Old Men

Unlike the Thanksgiving turkeys they pardoned, most ex-presidents live long and happy lives. All get a pension and Secret Service protection for them and their spouses. (Before Congress stepped up and provided a pension to presidential widows, steel millionaire Andrew Carnegie donated a pension to ex–first ladies.)

Gerald Ford lived to be our oldest ex-president: ninety-three and a half years old!

John Adams was so cheesed off at being voted out of office that he didn't even attend the inauguration of his rival, former friend Thomas Jefferson. Luckily, the two made up in 1812 and spent the last fourteen years of their lives, up until Adams's nineties, trading letters as close friends.

Herbert Hoover helped found and run the Boys Club of America, and at age eighty-three wrote a popular biography of Woodrow Wilson.

Likewise, **Jimmy Carter** became a novelist at age eighty with *The Hornet's Nest*, a book about the Revolutionary War.

Harry Truman attended Disneyland in his seventies—but refused to ride on Dumbo, since the elephant is a Republican Party symbol!

The Megabucks Stop Here

Truman refused to capitalize on his ex-president status, living for a time on nothing but his old army pension, $112.56 a month. But other ex-presidents have had no problem taking big checks. Bill Clinton makes an average of $189,000 every time he gives a speech! And Ronald Reagan took in a whopping $2 million for his first post–White House lectures, in Japan.

Term Limits

But death comes to ex-presidents, as it does to all men. Sometimes the end isn't unexpected. Ulysses Grant smoked twenty cigars a day, and died of throat

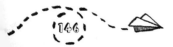

cancer. Franklin Pierce, on the other hand, was a heavy drinker—"the hero of many a well-fought bottle," as his Whig opponents called him. "There's nothing left but to get drunk," he said upon leaving the White House. Sure enough, twelve years later he was dead, from cirrhosis of the liver.

Other presidential deaths were more unexpected, like when Franklin Roosevelt slumped over from a stroke while having his portrait painted. The portrait remained unfinished. A couple of deaths even seemed suspicious. Warren Harding's wife refused to allow an autopsy on his body, which led to rumors that she had killed him! Likewise, Zachary Taylor's death was long attributed to eating "cherries and ice-cold milk on a hot day," but in 1991, his body was actually dug up to see if he'd been poisoned. No traces of arsenic were found, so watch out for those cherries, Junior Geniuses.

Extra Credit

When Teddy Roosevelt died in 1919, vice president Thomas Marshall commented, "Death had to take Roosevelt sleeping, for if he had been awake, there would have been a fight!"

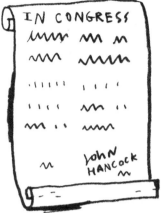

July 4, 1826, was the fiftieth anniversary of the signing of the Declaration of Independence. John Adams passed away that very night, supposedly after saying, "Thomas Jefferson survives." Unbeknownst to Adams, Jefferson had died a few hours earlier, on the very same historic day! Five years later, another founding father, James Monroe, also died on the Fourth of July. In the summer of 1836, James Madison was on his deathbed and was offered drugs to try to prolong his life to July 4, like his three fellow Founding Father presidents, but he refused and died in late June.

But no president timed his death like George Washington, who passed away late on December 14, 1799. He died during . . . the last hour . . . of the last day of the week . . . during the last month . . . of the last year of his century.

His last words were "'Tis well."

Who's Buried in Grant's Tomb?

When contestants were really struggling on the old game show *You Bet Your Life*, host Groucho Marx would give them a really easy question, like "What color is an orange?" His very favorite question was "Who's buried in Grant's tomb?"

All thirty-something dead presidents rest in peace, just like Grant, but some of their grave sites are more interesting than others.

Woodrow Wilson is the only president not buried in one of the fifty states. He's in the National Cathedral in Washington, D.C.

Andrew Johnson was buried with his head resting on a copy of the U.S. Constitution.

Abraham Lincoln's body has been moved seventeen times and his coffin opened six times since it was first laid to rest! (Mostly for security reasons. In 1876, a Chicago crime gang planned to steal Lincoln's body and hold it for a $200,000 ransom.)

Thomas Jefferson designed his own grave marker, mentioning three of his accomplishments: writing the Declaration of Independence, drafting a Virginia law for religious freedom, and founding the University of Virginia. That's right: Jefferson was so talented that he could leave "President of the United States" off his tombstone! Maybe he should have added, "Inventor of the humblebrag."

By the way, Groucho expected contestants to say that "President Grant" is buried in Grant's tomb, but I think you Junior Geniuses should know the real answer. For one thing, it's not just President Grant in the tomb—his wife, Julia, is there as well. Secondly, nobody is *buried* there at all—the tomb is a big marble chamber located *above* the ground.

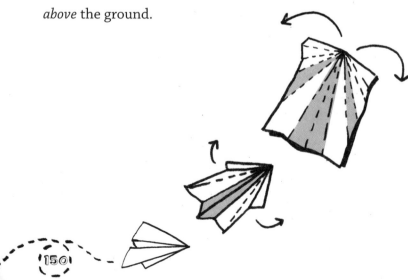

OFFICIAL JUNIOR GENIUS CERTIFICATION EXAM

NAME : _____

DATE : _____

This is the moment of truth, class—election night, if you will. Are you now an expert on the American presidency? Will you prove as nimble as a Jefferson or as dull-witted as a Harding? Get a number 2 pencil ready and turn the page when I say "Begin."

Wait for it.

Wait for it . . .

BEGIN.

1. James Buchanan was the only president who didn't have what?

Ⓐ A wife
Ⓑ An inaugural parade

Ⓒ A vice president
Ⓓ A college degree

2. According to the Constitution, how old must the president be?

Ⓐ 30 or older
Ⓑ 35 or older

Ⓒ 40 or older
Ⓓ 45 or older

3. What disease robbed Franklin Roosevelt of his ability to walk?

Ⓐ Polio
Ⓑ Addison's disease

Ⓒ Tuberculosis
Ⓓ Scarlet fever

4. Which Founding Father did *not* die on the Fourth of July?

Ⓐ John Adams
Ⓑ Thomas Jefferson

Ⓒ James Madison
Ⓓ James Monroe

5. What did Jimmy Carter grow on his family farm?

Ⓐ Cotton
Ⓑ Onions

Ⓒ Peaches
Ⓓ Peanuts

6. In a presidential motorcade, what's the code name for the president's limo?

Ⓐ Stagecoach   Ⓑ Chariot

Ⓒ Flagship   Ⓓ Payload

7. Harrison, Tyler, Taylor, and Fillmore were the only presidents from what political party?

Ⓐ Federalist   Ⓑ Free Soil

Ⓒ Greenback   Ⓓ Whig

8. What was Abraham Lincoln doing the night he was shot?

Ⓐ Taking a walk   Ⓑ Catching a train

Ⓒ Seeing a play   Ⓓ Visiting a hospital

9. Why was Rutherford Hayes's wife nicknamed "Lemonade Lucy"?

Ⓐ She was sour and mean   Ⓑ She didn't drink alcohol

Ⓒ She dressed all in yellow   Ⓓ She introduced lemonade to America

10. Who was the oldest president, almost seventy at his swearing-in?

Ⓐ Andrew Jackson   Ⓑ Gerald Ford

Ⓒ Ronald Reagan   Ⓓ George H. W. Bush

11. During what war was the White House badly burned?

    Ⓐ Mexican-American
       War
    Ⓑ Civil War

    Ⓒ Black Hawk War
    Ⓓ War of 1812

12. The president's desk is built from the old timbers of what?

    Ⓐ A ship
    Ⓑ A railway bridge

    Ⓒ A cavalry fort
    Ⓓ A log cabin

13. George Washington and seven other presidents were born in what state?

    Ⓐ Massachusetts
    Ⓑ Ohio

    Ⓒ Virginia
    Ⓓ Pennsylvania

14. Jefferson kept a pair of what unusual pets on the White House lawn?

    Ⓐ Cougars
    Ⓑ Giant tortoises

    Ⓒ Grizzly bears
    Ⓓ Mountain goats

15. Which of these was the brainchild of the Eisenhower administration?

    Ⓐ Interstate highways
    Ⓑ Hoover Dam

    Ⓒ Daylight saving time
    Ⓓ the Panama Canal

16. What symbol of war does the eagle on the presidential seal carry?

Ⓐ A lightning bolt   Ⓑ A shield

Ⓒ Arrows   Ⓓ Three swords

17. Who explored the Amazon after leaving the White House?

Ⓐ Ulysses S. Grant   Ⓑ Teddy Roosevelt

Ⓒ Woodrow Wilson   Ⓓ Harry Truman

18. What was wrong with William Henry Harrison's inauguration speech?

Ⓐ He forgot to give one   Ⓑ It was too long

Ⓒ He was drunk   Ⓓ It was mostly in Dutch

19. Who was inspired to run for office when he met JFK as a boy?

Ⓐ Jimmy Carter   Ⓑ Bill Clinton

Ⓒ George W. Bush   Ⓓ Barack Obama

20. Since 1878, the White House lawn has hosted families celebrating what holiday?

Ⓐ Valentine's Day   Ⓑ Mother's Day

Ⓒ Halloween   Ⓓ Easter

All right, pencils down! Turn the page to the answers and see how you did.

ANSWERS

1. △	2. ▢	3. △	4. ◁	5. ▢
6. △	7. ▢	8. ◁	9. ▢	10. ◁
11. ▢	12. △	13. ◁	14. ◁	15. △
16. ◁	17. ▢	18. ▢	19. ▢	20. ◁

Scoring

16–20	Certified Junior Genius!
13–15	Unimpeachably Close
10–12	Inaugural Ballpark
6–9	Mount Blush-more
0–5	Fail to the Chief

Did you get them "oll korrect," Junior Genius? Well done! Go to JuniorGeniusGuides.com to print out your official certificate.

If not, don't worry—*you can keep taking the test until you do!* Grover Cleveland lost the electoral college by a whisker in 1888, but did he go crying back to, uh, Albany or someplace? *He did not.* He ran again in 1892, against the same guy . . . and won. If you like knowing stuff well enough to keep plugging away, I bet you're Junior Genius material.

HOMEWORK

If today's lesson has left you breathless for *yet more information* about the presidents of the United States— if you're still chanting, "Four more years! Four more years!"—well, that's what I like to hear. Here are some projects I recommend to anyone looking for a "new deal."

○ **WAX POETIC.** Does the leader of the free world inspire you to write free verse? Try an acrostic poem. Write a president's name down the side of your paper, and then start each line of your poem with one letter of his name. Here's how my "Ode to Calvin Coolidge" begins:

> **C oolidge, how thou left Vermont's bright glade**
> **A nd made th' exalted White House thy true home!**
> **L ounged endlessly in bed and servants bade**
> **V aseline to smear on thy be-wrinkled dome . . .**

Oh, wow, that is good stuff. I'm getting patriotic shivers.

○ **TAKE A FIELD TRIP.** One of the best things about being president is all the random stuff that gets named for you. Counties, babies, highways, government buildings—the sky's the limit! There's now a tiny Mexican desert beetle named for Theodore Roosevelt and an asteroid named for Herbert Hoover. Grab a map or a phone book and see how many places named f o r presidents you can visit in your state. Keep a checklist, like a bird-watcher!

○ **FOLLOW THE MONEY.** If you poke around in your parents' pockets, junk drawers, and purses, you can find lots of presidents—on tiny metal disks and green paper rectangles. *Get permission first, of course!* But see how many different presidents you can find. I doubt you'll be seeing *these* bills! They're still officially legal, but haven't been printed since 1945:

○ **DROP HIM A LINE.** The president represents the American people—why not let your voice be heard? Write him a note at www.whitehouse.gov/contact, or even the old-fashioned way—with an envelope and stamp and everything!—at The White House, 1600 Pennsylvania Avenue NW, Washington, D.C. 20500. The president probably won't ban homework or repeal spinach at your request, but some kids have been known to get replies from the Oval Office!

THE FINAL BELL

Class: Would you like to travel to . . .

○ a planet where a day is longer than a year?

○ a white dwarf star whose core is a giant diamond, over 10 billion trillion trillion carats in weight?

○ a hurricane twice the size of Earth that's been raging for centuries?

Our next class together will be **Ken Jennings' Junior Genius Guides: Outer Space.** I'll see you then. Bring your brain and a nice, shiny apple for the teacher. I also accept other produce and gift baskets.

But even when we're not together, friends, you can be learning every day. Always remember the Junior Genius slogan, coined by a famous seventeenth-century Génie Petit (that's a French Junior Genius) named Blaise Pascal: "It is much better to know something about everything than everything about something."

Class dismissed!

23

BENJAMIN
HARRISON

24

GROVER
CLEVELAND

25

WILLIAM
McKINLEY

26

THEODORE
ROOSEVELT

27

WILLIAM HOWARD
TAFT

28

WOODROW
WILSON

29

WARREN G.
HARDING

30

CALVIN
COOLIDGE

31

HERBERT
HOOVER

32

FRANKLIN D.
ROOSEVELT

33

HARRY S.
TRUMAN